Price $7.50

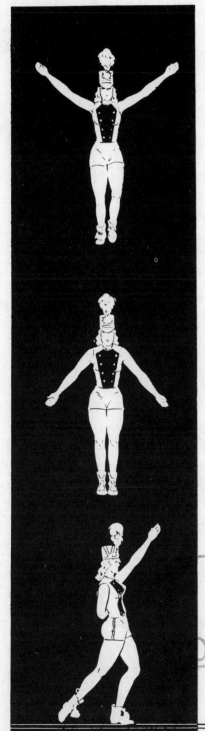

PHALANX

DRILL

MOVEMENTS

A. R. Casavant

Copyright © 1959
Southern Music Company
P. O. Box 329
San Antonio, Texas

FOREWORD

"If a man makes a better mousetrap"—you know the rest. Through the grades from six to twelve Albert R. Casavant displayed the energy, the intelligence, and the ability to take pains, which leads to excellence. Those same attributes and his later experience has produced, in this series of books, a system of precision marching which is fundamental and outstanding. The essential clarity of his presentation makes it possible to demand, and accomplish, the best from any marching group.

Charles F. Corlett
Supervising Instructor of Instrumental Music
Warren, Ohio.

This book is dedicated to the high school bands of the United States with a special salute to the Warren G. Harding High School Band of Warren, Ohio.

The memories of the wonderful experiences we had as students in these bands will always be with us.

Thanks, a million, Mr. Corlett.

A. R. Casavant

TABLE OF CONTENTS

DRILL KEY

A

STANDING POSITIONS (Attention, Marktime, Freeze, etc.)

B

FORWARD MOVEMENT

C

OBLIQUE MOVEMENTS

D

BACKWARD MOVEMENT

E

SIDE STEP OR SHIFT MOVEMENT

F

TURNS

START AND/OR FINISH OF DRILL MOVEMENT

Sticks

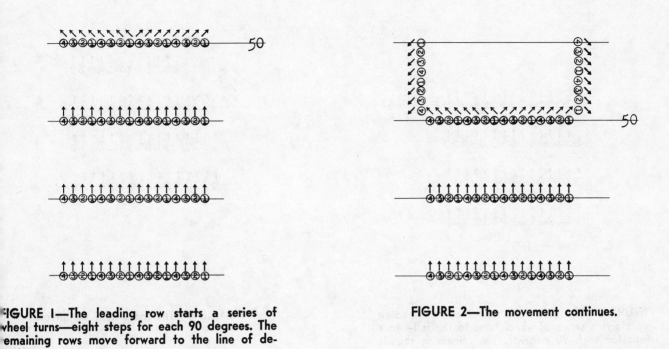

FIGURE I—The leading row starts a series of wheel turns—eight steps for each 90 degrees. The remaining rows move forward to the line of departure.

FIGURE 2—The movement continues.

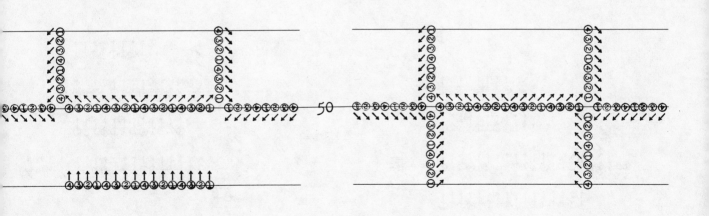

FIGURE 3—The movement continues.

FIGURE 4—The movement continues.

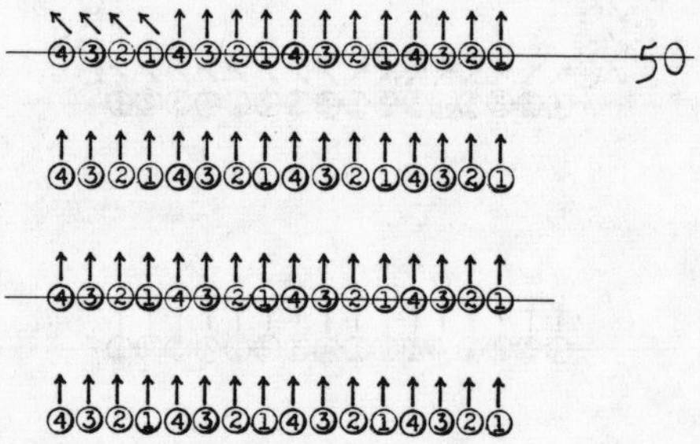

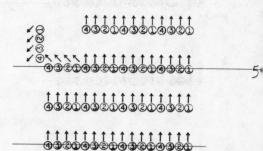

50

FIGURE 5—The left flank squad of the leading row starts a series of wheel turns to the left—four steps for each 90 degrees. The remaining squads move forward to their lines of departure.

FIGURE 6—The movement continues.

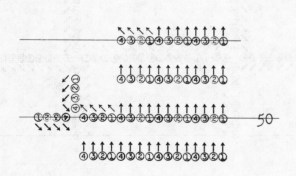

50

FIGURE 7—The movement continues.

50

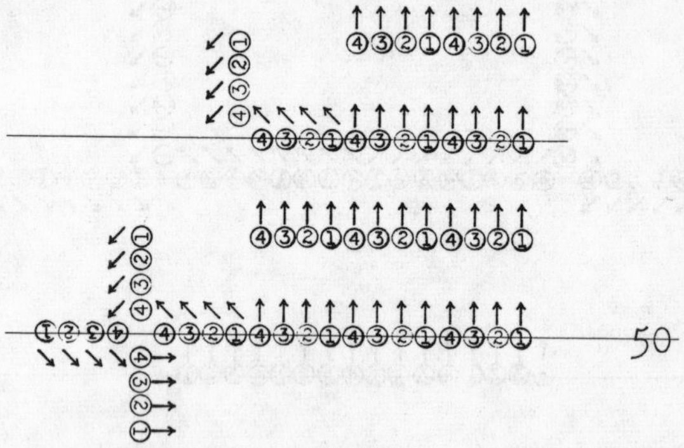

FIGURE 8—The movement continues.

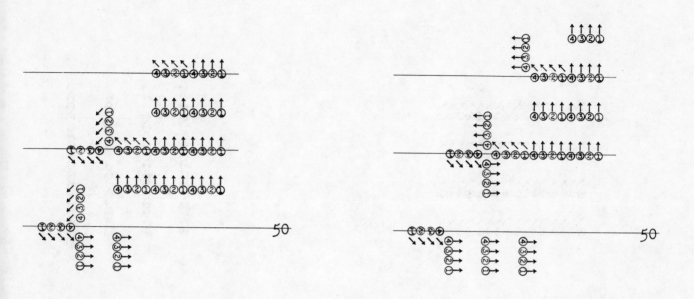

FIGURE 9—The movement continues.

FIGURE 10—The movement continues.

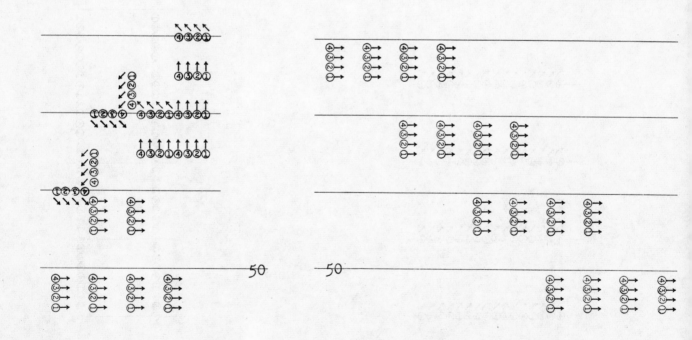

FIGURE 11—The movement continues.

FIGURE 12—The movement continues.

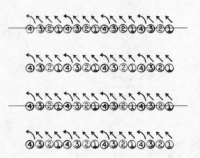

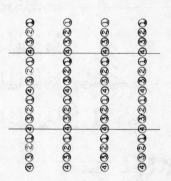

FIGURE 13—Each squad executes squads left.

FIGURE 14—The movement is complete.

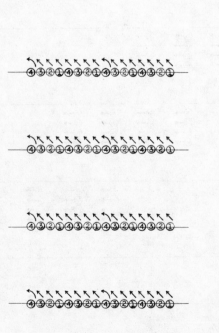

FIGURE 15—Each double squad executes a 90 degree turn.

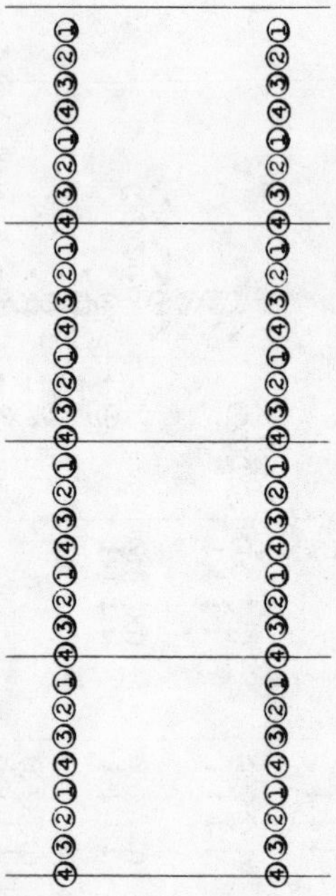

FIGURE 16—The movement is complete.

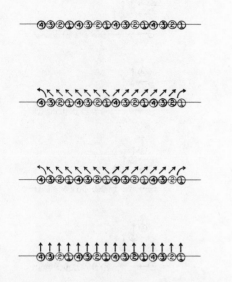

FIGURE 17—The leading row holds. The second and third rows split and turn to the outside. The last row moves forward eight steps.

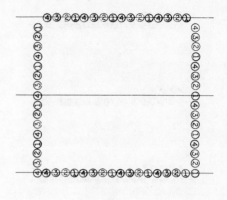

FIGURE 18—The movement is complete.

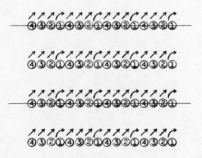

FIGURE 19—Each squad executes a 45 degree squad turn and adjusts the interval.

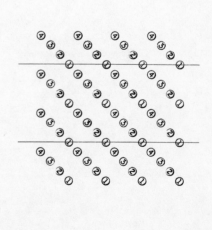

FIGURE 20—The movement is complete.

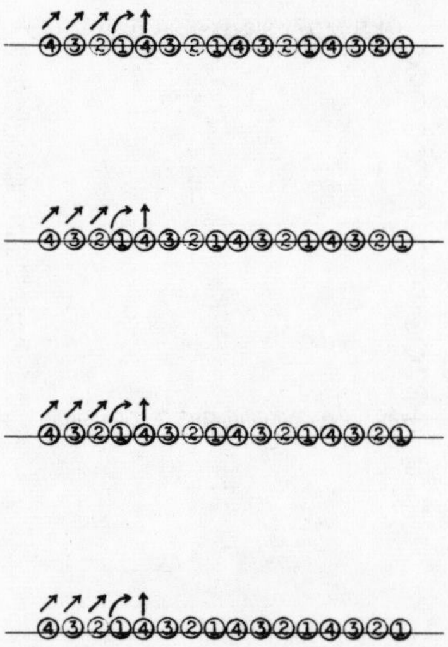

FIGURE 21—The left flank squad of each row executes squad right and forward. The remaining members of the rows peel from the left.

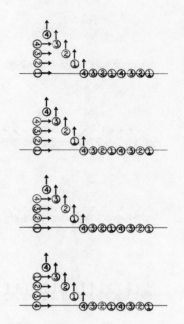

FIGURE 22—The movement continues.

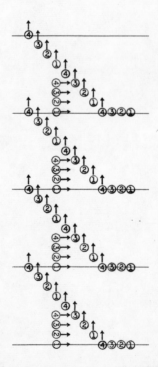

FIGURE 23—The movement continues.

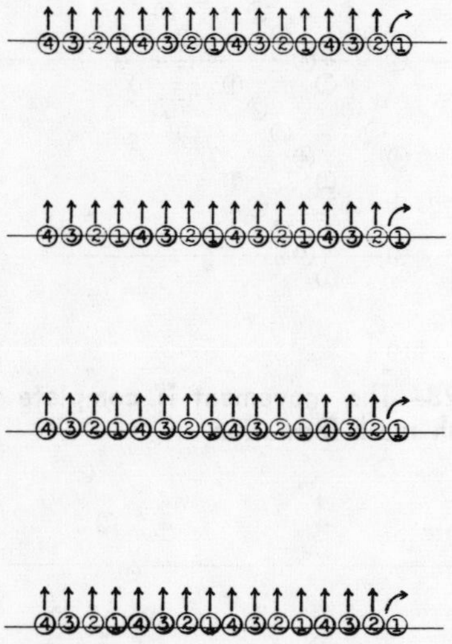

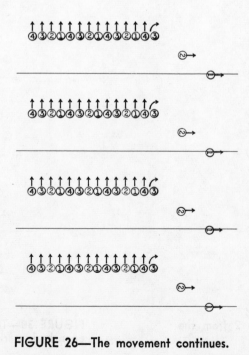

FIGURE 24—Each row executes flank 2 from the right to the right.

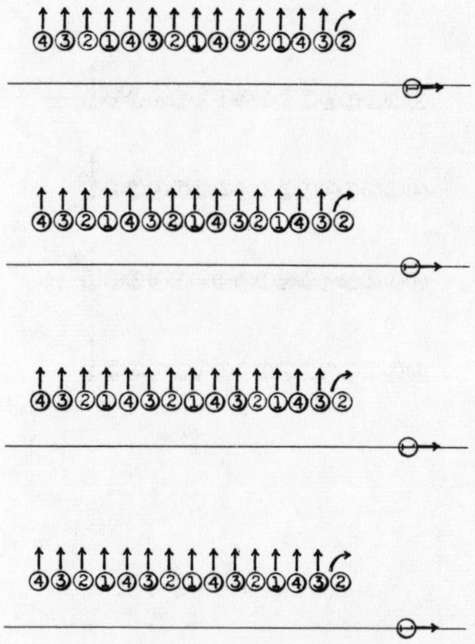

FIGURE 25—The movement continues.

FIGURE 26—The movement continues.

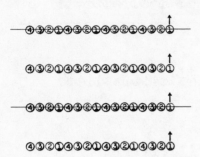

FIGURE 27—Each row executes a peel from the right.

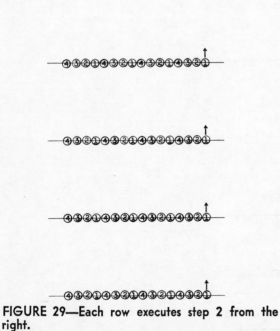

FIGURE 29—Each row executes step 2 from the right.

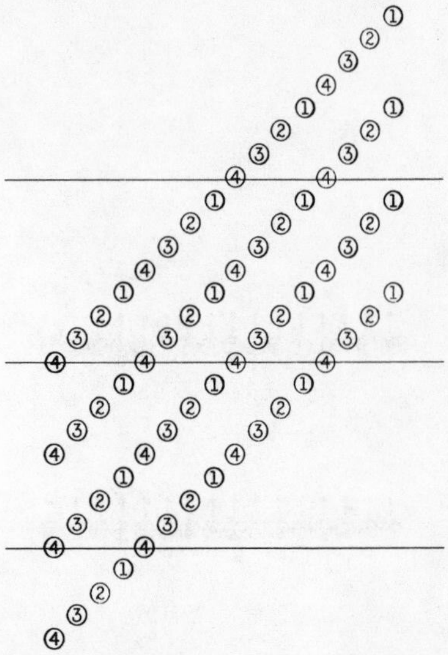

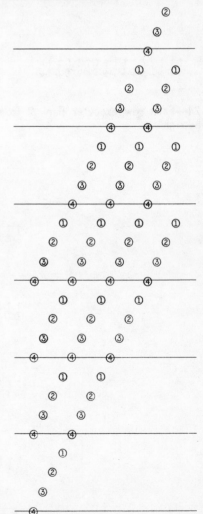

FIGURE 28—The movement is complete with the closed hash mark formation.

FIGURE 30—The movement is complete with the open hash mark formation.

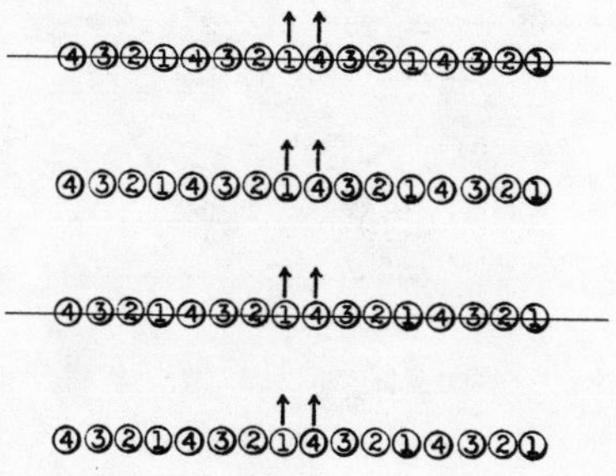

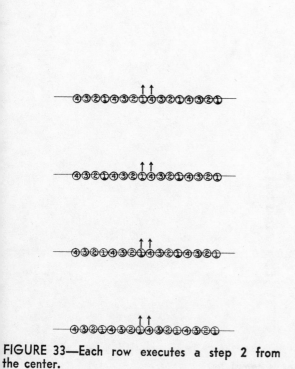

FIGURE 31—Each row executes a peel from the center.

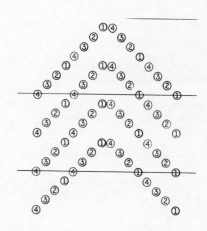

FIGURE 32—The movement is complete with the closed chevron formation.

FIGURE 33—Each row executes a step 2 from the center.

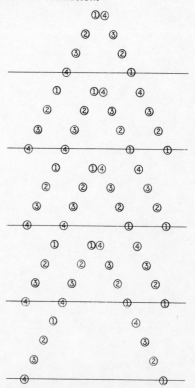

FIGURE 34—The movement is complete with the open chevron formation.

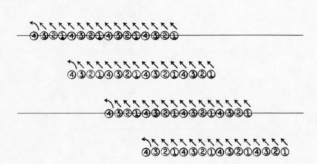

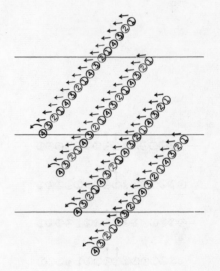

FIGURE 35—The unit is in staggered formation. Each row executes a wheel turn.

FIGURE 36—The movement continues.

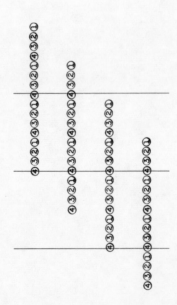

FIGURE 37—The movement is complete.

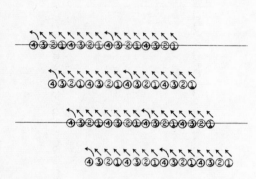

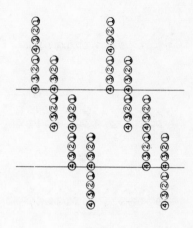

FIGURE 38—The unit is in staggered formation. Each half row executes a wheel turn.

FIGURE 39—The movement is complete.

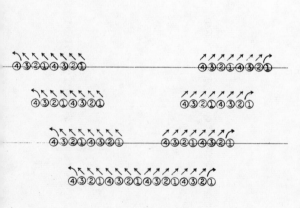

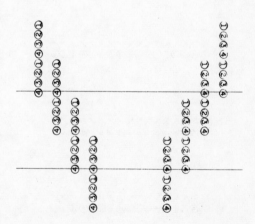

FIGURE 40—The unit is in a partially covered echelon formation. Each half row executes a wheel turn to the outside.

FIGURE 41—The movement is complete.

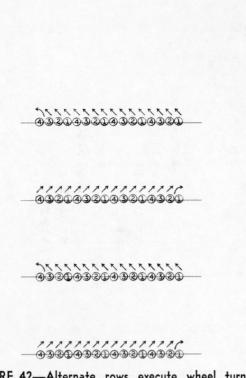

FIGURE 42—Alternate rows execute wheel turn to left and right.

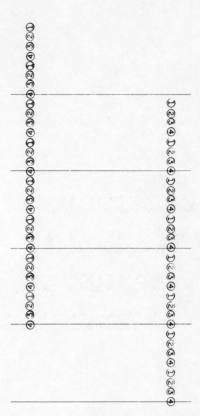

FIGURE 43—The movement is complete.

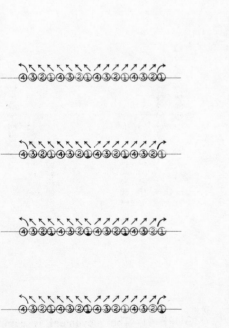

FIGURE 44—Each half row executes a wheel turn to the outside.

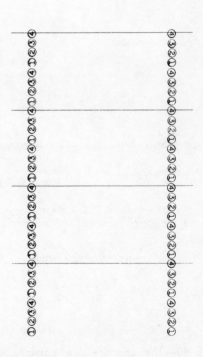

FIGURE 45—The movement is complete.

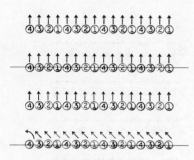

FIGURE 46—The last row executes a wheel turn. The remaining rows move forward to lines of departure.

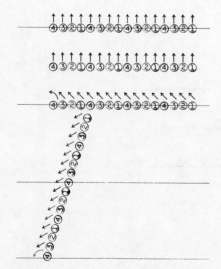

FIGURE 47—The movement continues.

FIGURE 48—The movement is complete.

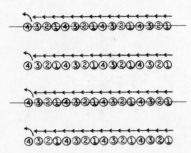

FIGURE 49—Each row side steps to line of departure. Individuals flank 2—turning 270 degrees to the outside or executing a compound turn of two 90 degree turns.

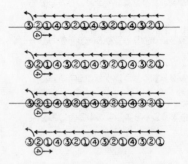

FIGURE 50—The movement continues.

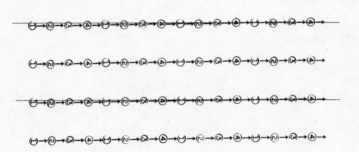

FIGURE 51—The movement is complete.

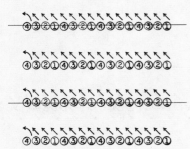

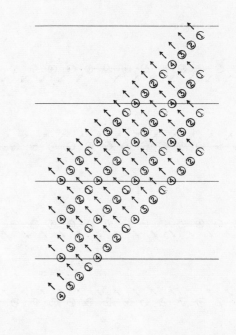

FIGURE 52—Each row executes a 45 degree wheel turn and moves in the new direction.

FIGURE 53—The movement continues.

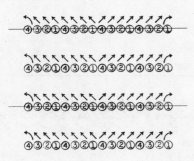

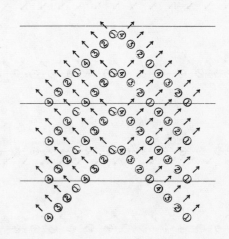

FIGURE 54—Each half row executes a 45 degree wheel turn to the outside and moves in the new direction.

FIGURE 55—The movement continues.

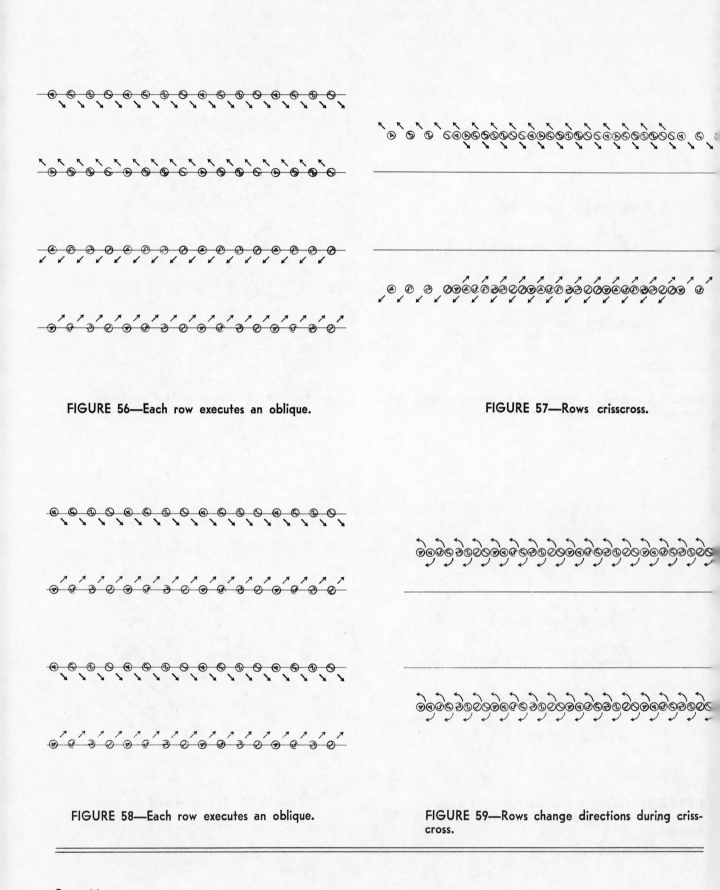

FIGURE 56—Each row executes an oblique.

FIGURE 57—Rows crisscross.

FIGURE 58—Each row executes an oblique.

FIGURE 59—Rows change directions during crisscross.

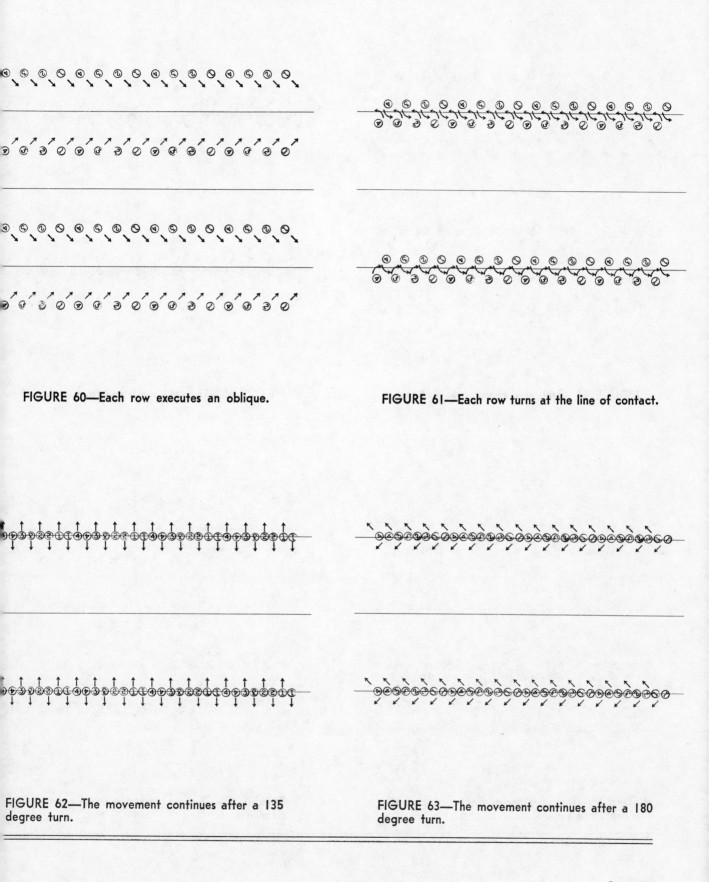

FIGURE 60—Each row executes an oblique.

FIGURE 61—Each row turns at the line of contact.

FIGURE 62—The movement continues after a 135 degree turn.

FIGURE 63—The movement continues after a 180 degree turn.

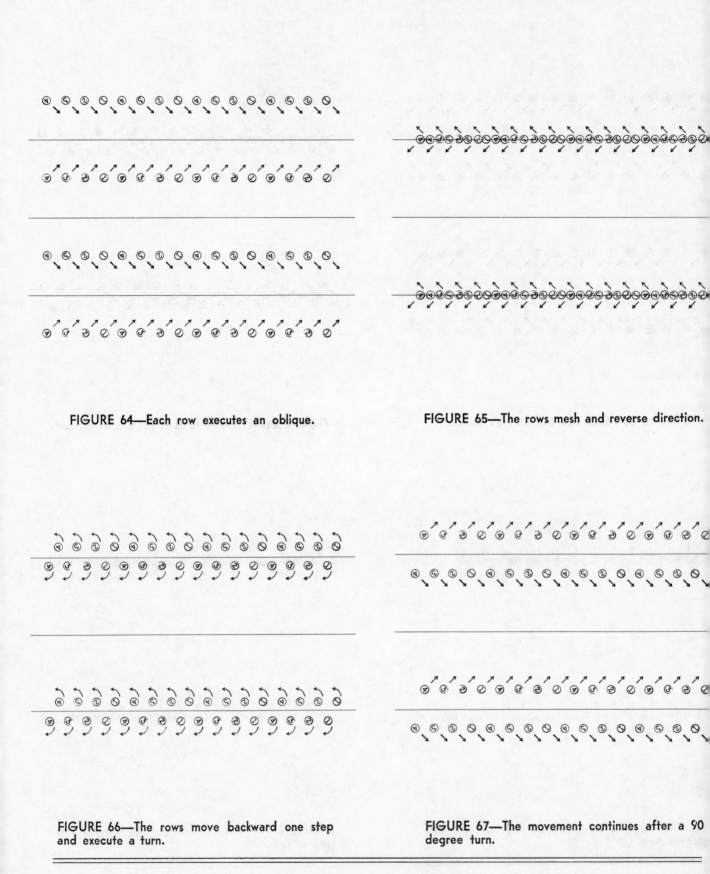

FIGURE 64—Each row executes an oblique.

FIGURE 65—The rows mesh and reverse direction.

FIGURE 66—The rows move backward one step and execute a turn.

FIGURE 67—The movement continues after a 90 degree turn.

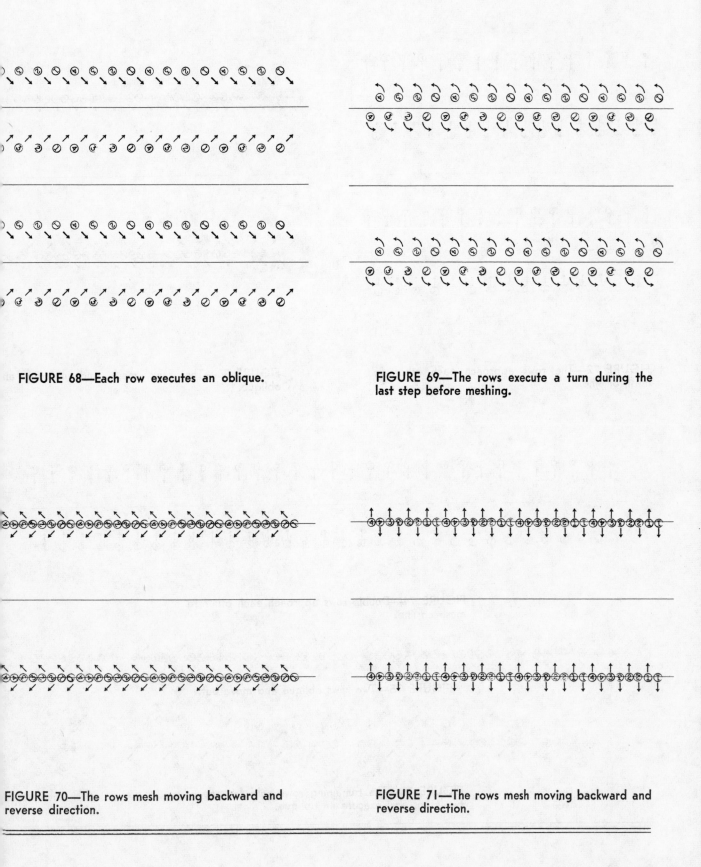

FIGURE 68—Each row executes an oblique.

FIGURE 69—The rows execute a turn during the last step before meshing.

FIGURE 70—The rows mesh moving backward and reverse direction.

FIGURE 71—The rows mesh moving backward and reverse direction.

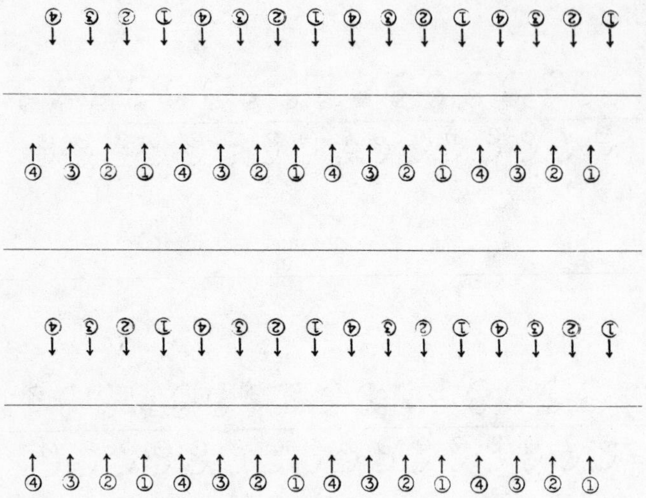

FIGURE 72—The rows approach each other to mesh on line.

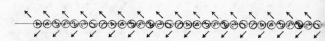

FIGURE 73—The rows mesh and execute an oblique.

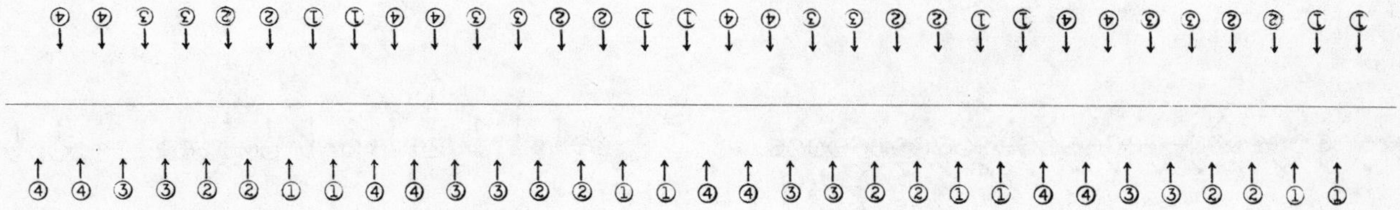

FIGURE 74—Double rows approach each other to mesh on line.

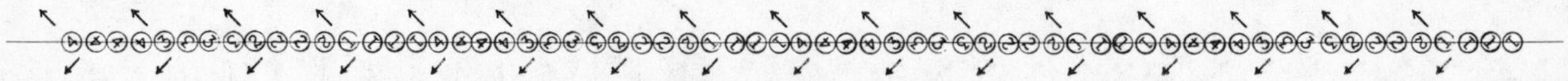

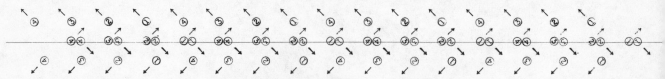

FIGURE 75—Two rows oblique and move out.

FIGURE 76—The remaining rows hold for one or two steps and execute an oblique.

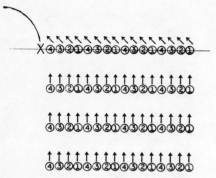

FIGURE 77—The leading row starts a wheel turn with the pivot moving on an arc. The remaining rows half step to the line of departure.

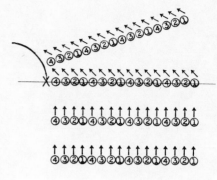

FIGURE 78—The movement continues.

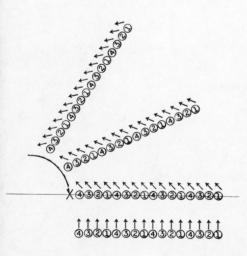

FIGURE 79—The movement continues.

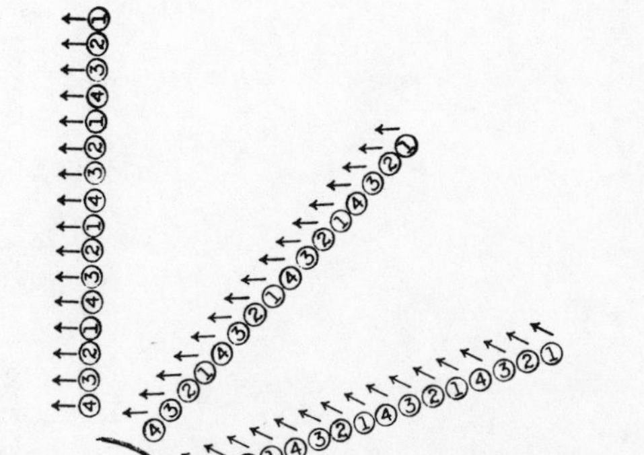

FIGURE 80—The movement continues.

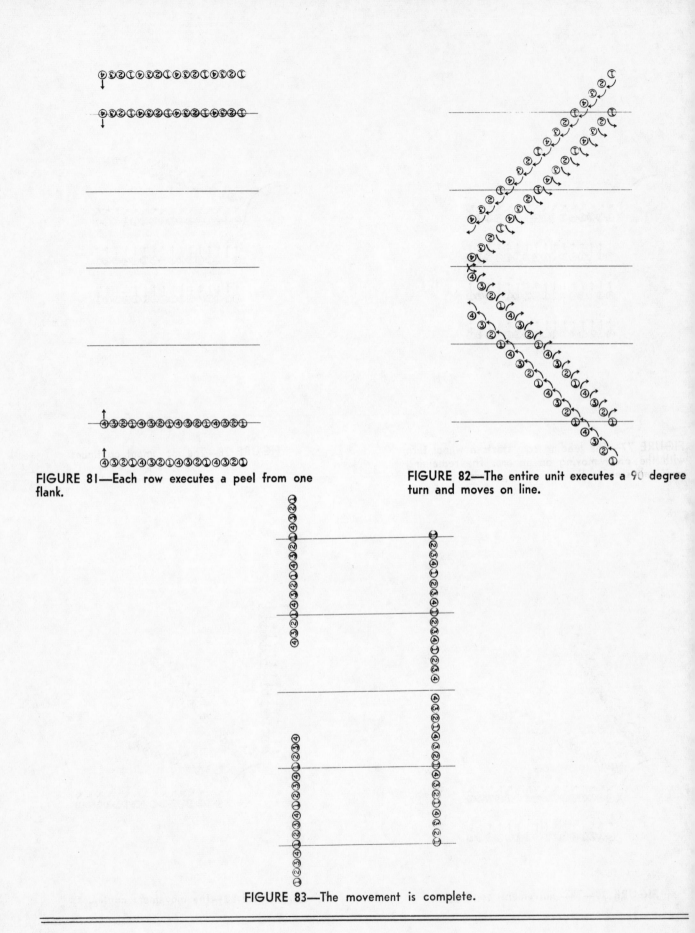

FIGURE 81—Each row executes a peel from one flank.

FIGURE 82—The entire unit executes a 90 degree turn and moves on line.

FIGURE 83—The movement is complete.

④③②①④③②①④③②①④③②①

④③②①④③②①④③②①④③②①

④③②①④③②①④③②①④③②①

④③②①④③②①④③②①④③②①

FIGURE 84—The unit is in staggered formation. The last row executes step 2.

④③②①④③②①④③②①④③②①

④③②①④③②①④③②①④③②①

④ ④③②①④③②①④③②①④③②①
③
②①④③②①④③②①④③②①

FIGURE 85—The third row starts step 2.

④③②①④③②①④③②①④③②①

④ ④ ④③②①④③②①④③②①④③②①
③ ③
② ② ①④③②①④③②①④③②①
①
④③②①④③②①④③②①

FIGURE 86—The second row starts step 2.

④ ④ ④ ④③②①④③②①④③②①④③②①
③ ③ ③
② ② ② ①④③②①④③②①④③②①
① ① ①
④ ④③②①④③②①④③②①
③
②①④③②①④③②①

FIGURE 87—The first row starts step 2.

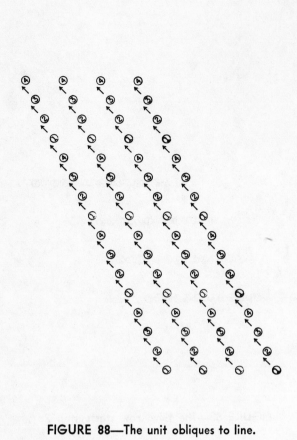

FIGURE 88—The unit obliques to line.

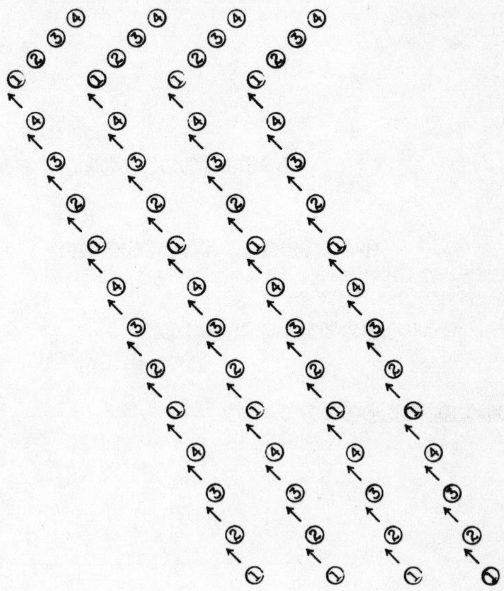

FIGURE 89—The movement continues.

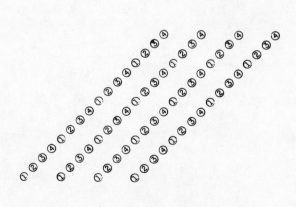

FIGURE 90—The movement is complete.

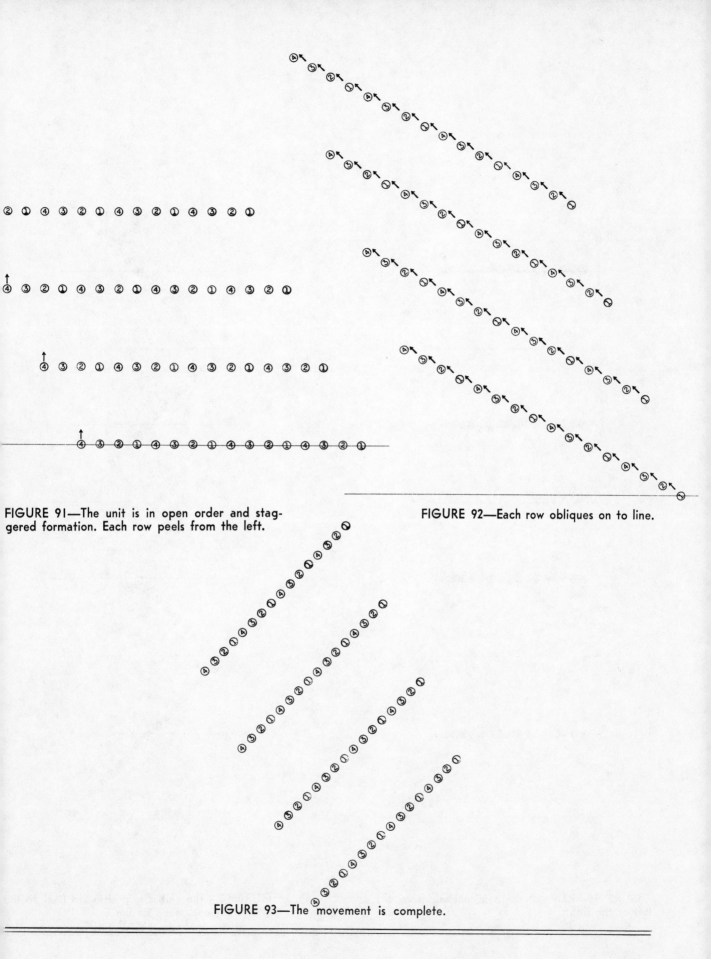

FIGURE 91—The unit is in open order and staggered formation. Each row peels from the left.

FIGURE 92—Each row obliques on to line.

FIGURE 93—The movement is complete.

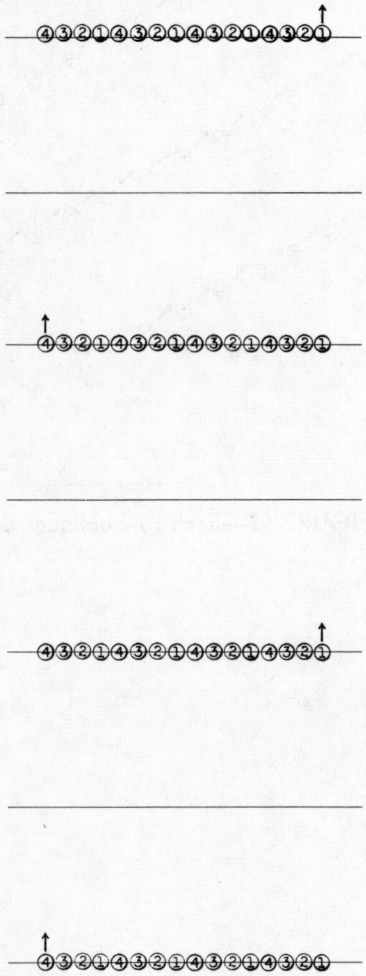

FIGURE 94—Rows alternate in peeling from the left or the right.

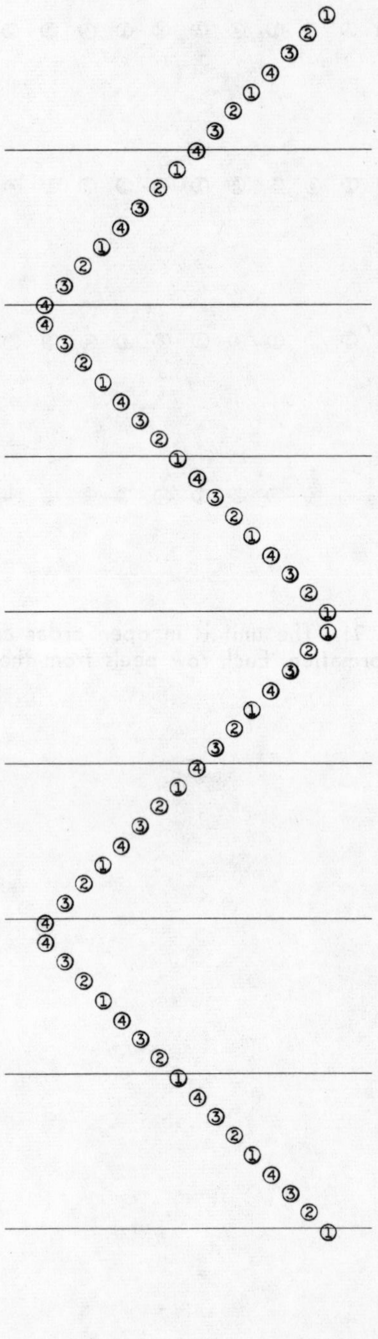

FIGURE 95—The unit is in position to flank to the left or right and move on line.

FIGURE 96—Each row executes step 2 from both ends.

FIGURE 97—The unit is in position to turn to left or right or to the center and mesh as the new line is formed.

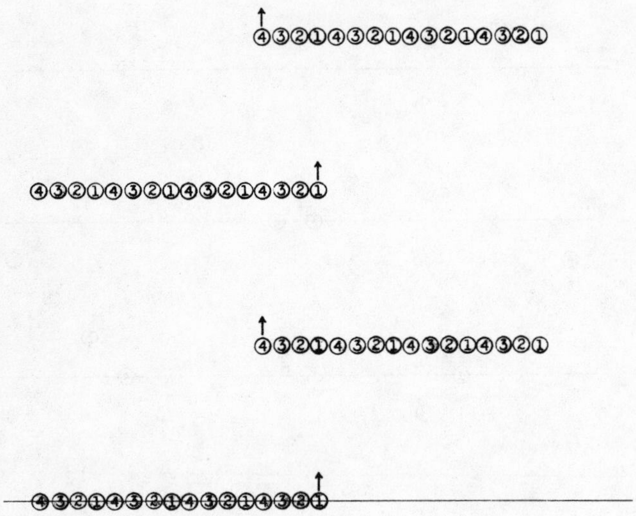

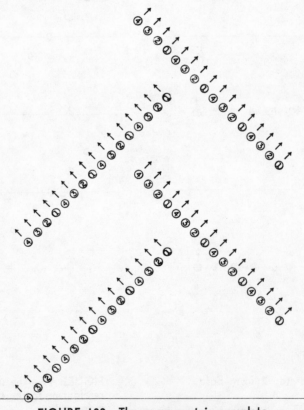

FIGURE 98—The rows are staggered. The rows alternate in peel from the left or from the right.

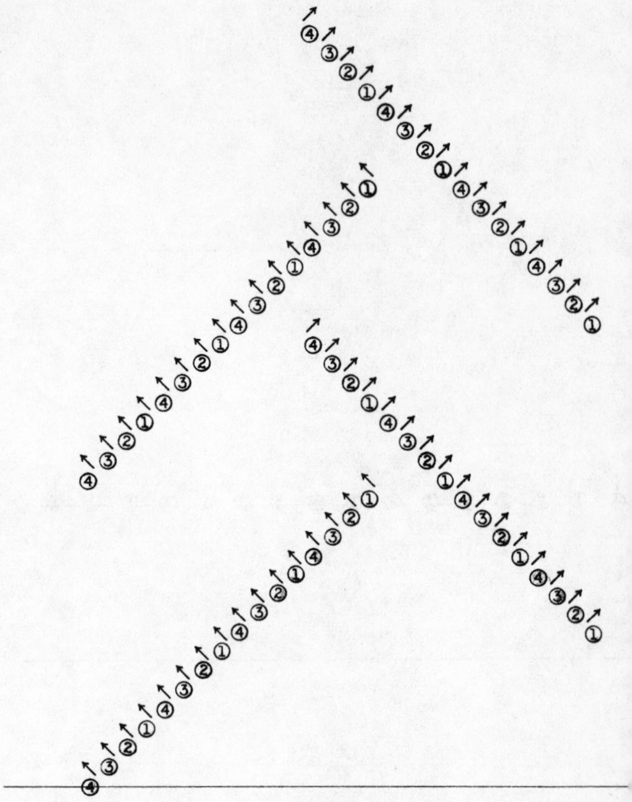

FIGURE 99—Each row turns 45 degrees to the outside.

FIGURE 100—The movement is complete.

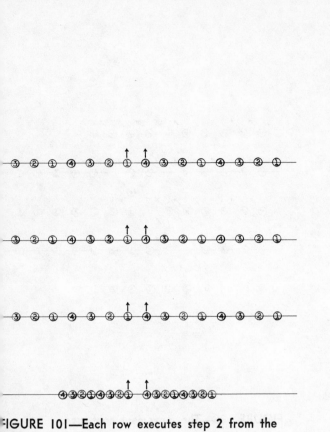

FIGURE 101—Each row executes step 2 from the center.

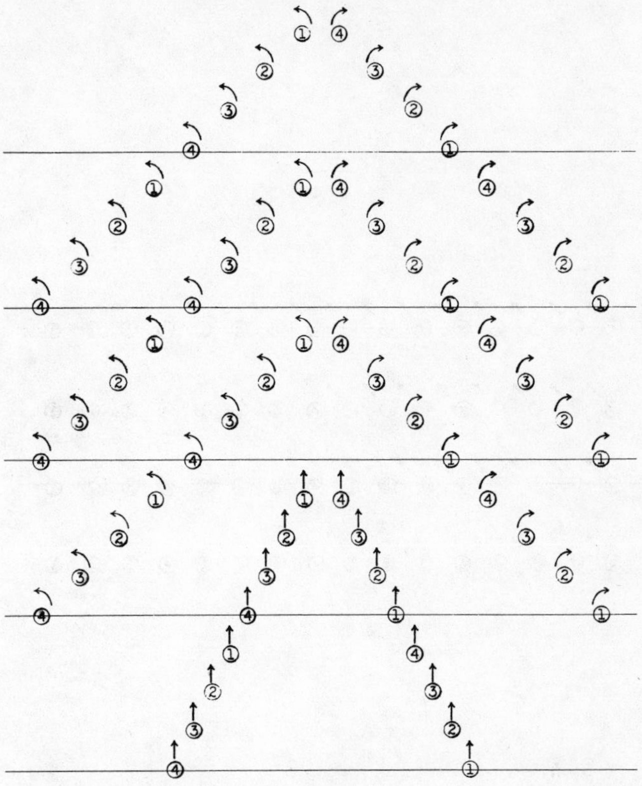

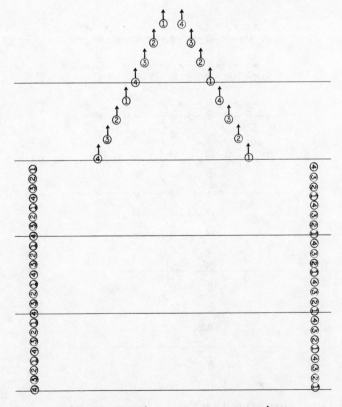

FIGURE 102—The first 3 rows execute 120 degree turns to the outside.

FIGURE 103—The movement is complete.

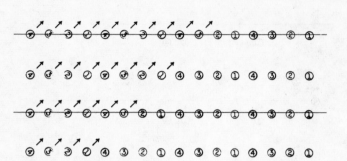

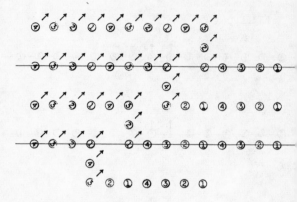

FIGURE 104—Each row executes step 2 from the left.

FIGURE 105—The movement continues.

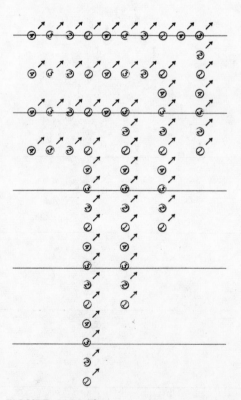

FIGURE 106—The movement is complete.

Pattern Drill

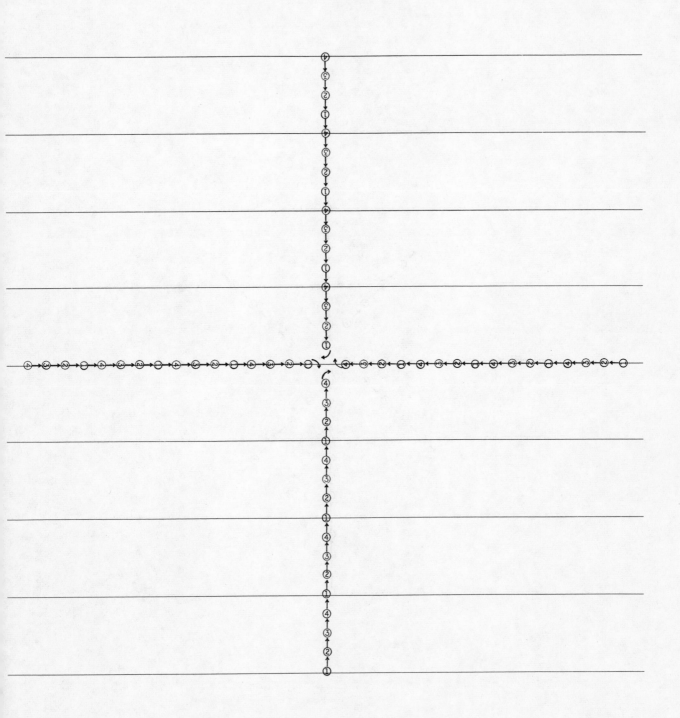

FIGURE 107—The unit is divided into four sections. Each section is in file and executes a column half right.

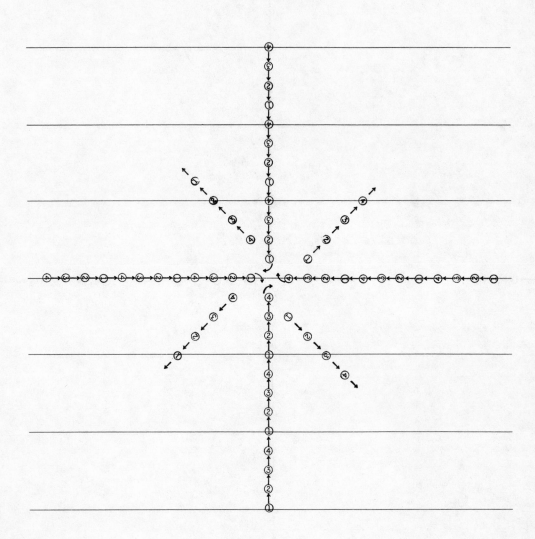

FIGURE 108—The movement continues.

FIGURE 109—The movement is complete.

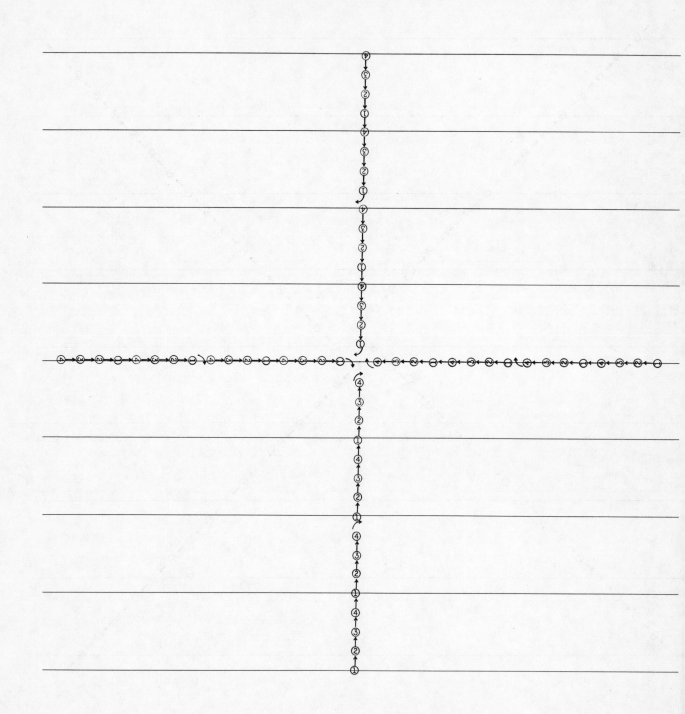

FIGURE 110—The unit is divided into four sections. Each section executes column half right.

FIGURE III—The movement is complete.

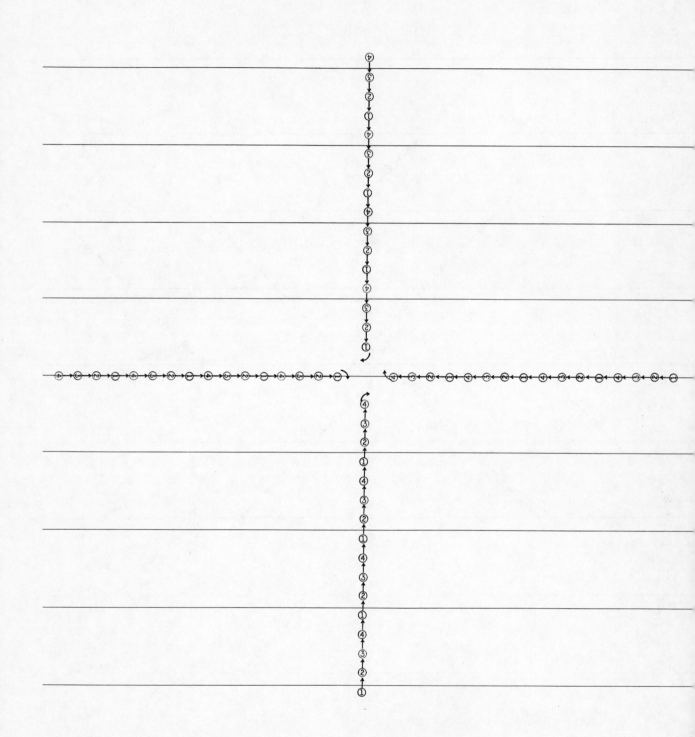

FIGURE 112—The unit is divided into four sections. Each section is in file and alternates its file in column half right and column half left.

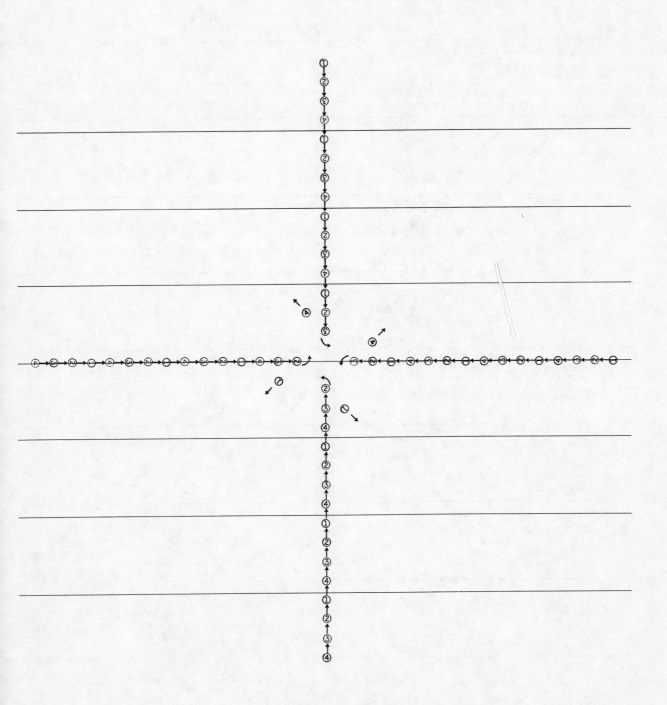

FIGURE 113—The movement continues.

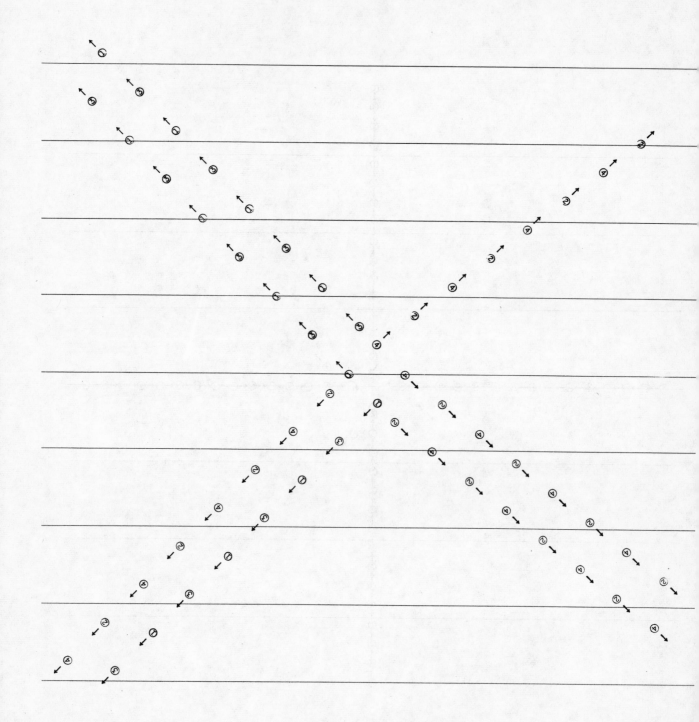

FIGURE 114—The movement is complete.

FIGURE 115—The unit is divided into four sections. Each section is in file and executes column half right.

FIGURE 116—The movement is complete.

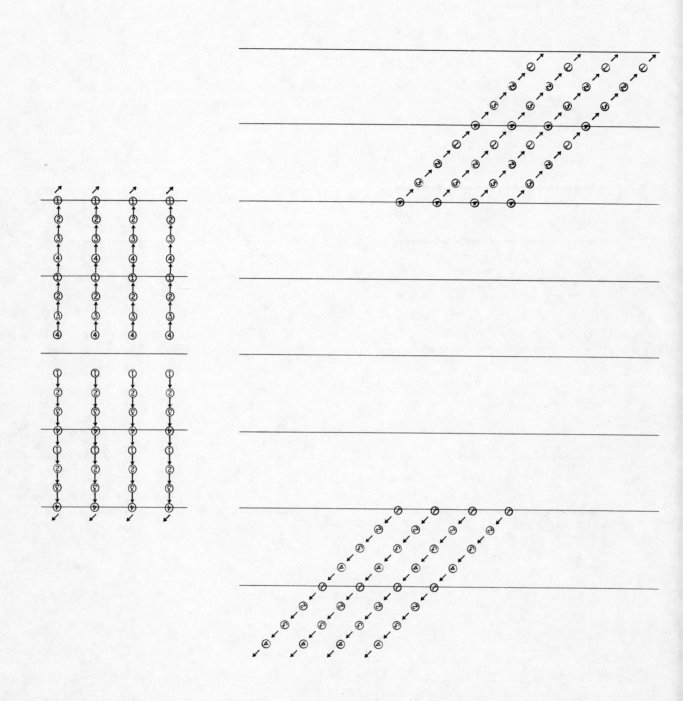

FIGURE 117—The unit is divided into eight sections. Each section is in file and executes column half right.

FIGURE 118—The movement is complete.

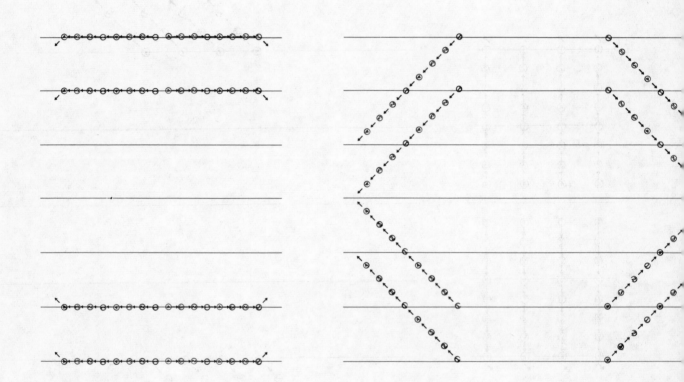

FIGURE 119—The unit is divided into eight sections. Each section is in file. Four sections execute column half right and four sections execute column half left.

FIGURE 120—The movement is complete.

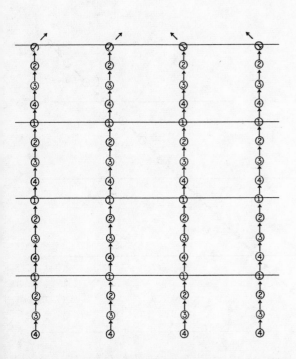

FIGURE 121—The unit is divided into four sections. Each section is in file and executes a column half right or column half left. Each file changes direction every four steps.

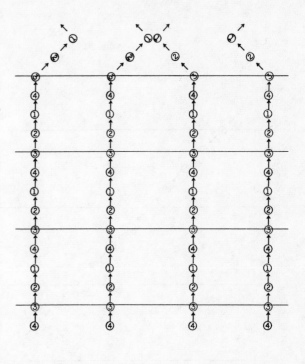

FIGURE 122—The movement continues.

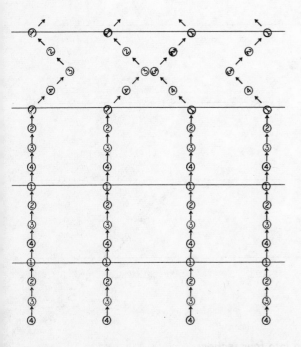

FIGURE 123—The movement continues.

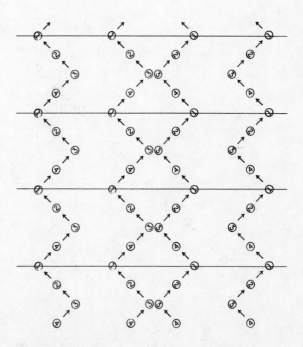

FIGURE 124—The movement continues.

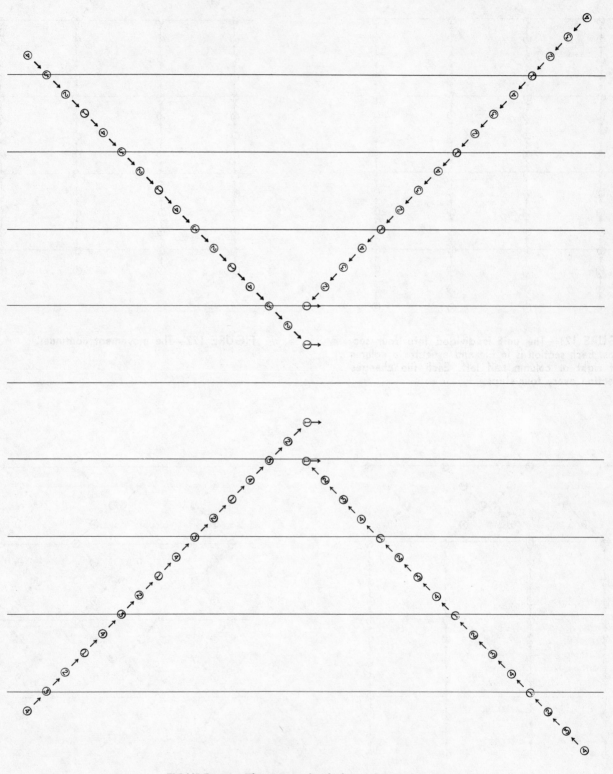

FIGURE 125—The unit is divided into four sections.
Each section is in file.

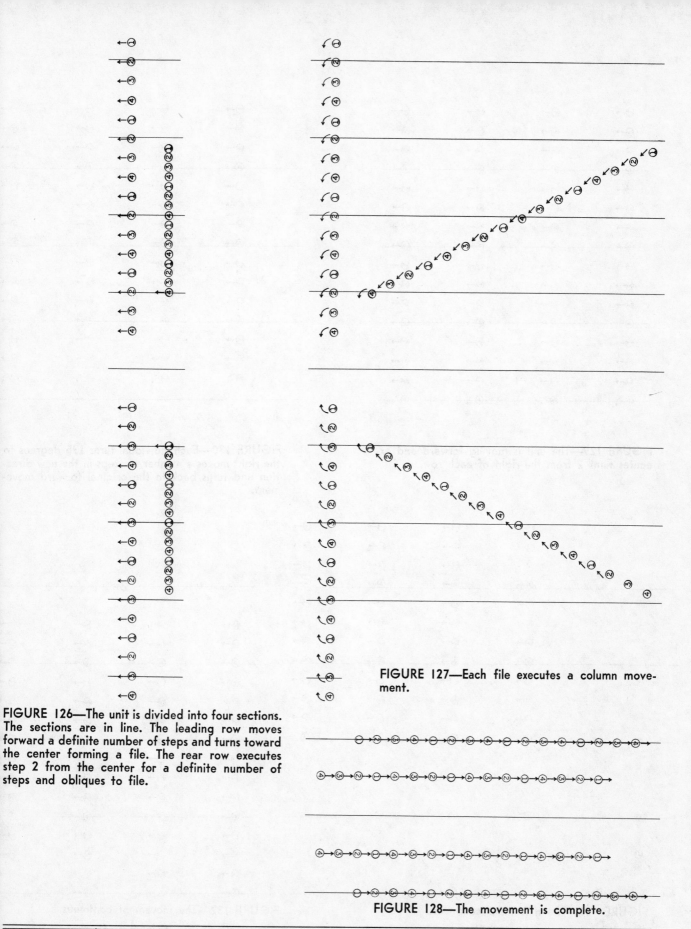

FIGURE 126—The unit is divided into four sections. The sections are in line. The leading row moves forward a definite number of steps and turns toward the center forming a file. The rear row executes step 2 from the center for a definite number of steps and obliques to file.

FIGURE 127—Each file executes a column movement.

FIGURE 128—The movement is complete.

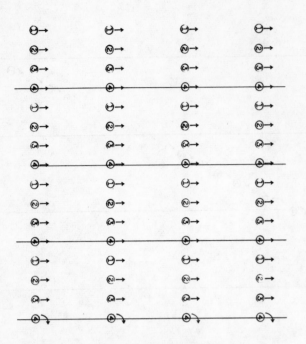

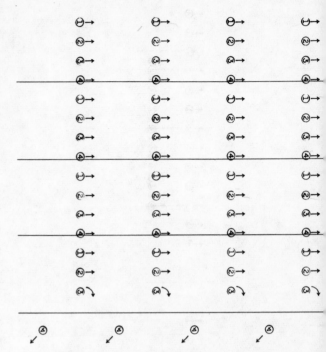

FIGURE 129—The unit is moving forward and executes flank 2 from the right of each row.

FIGURE 130—Each individual turns 135 degrees to the right moves a number of steps in the new direction and turns back to the original forward movement.

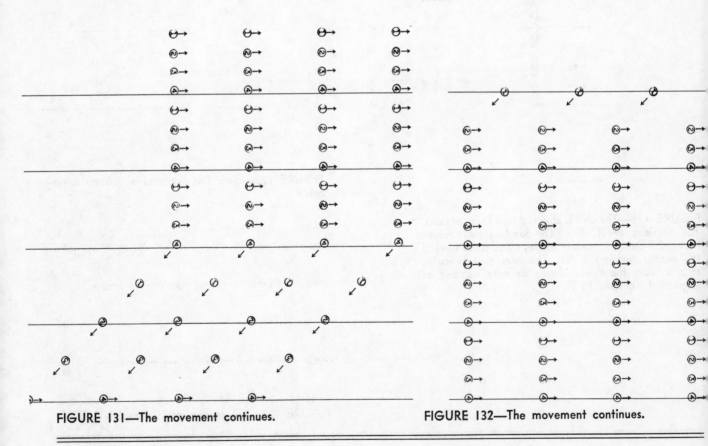

FIGURE 131—The movement continues.

FIGURE 132—The movement continues.

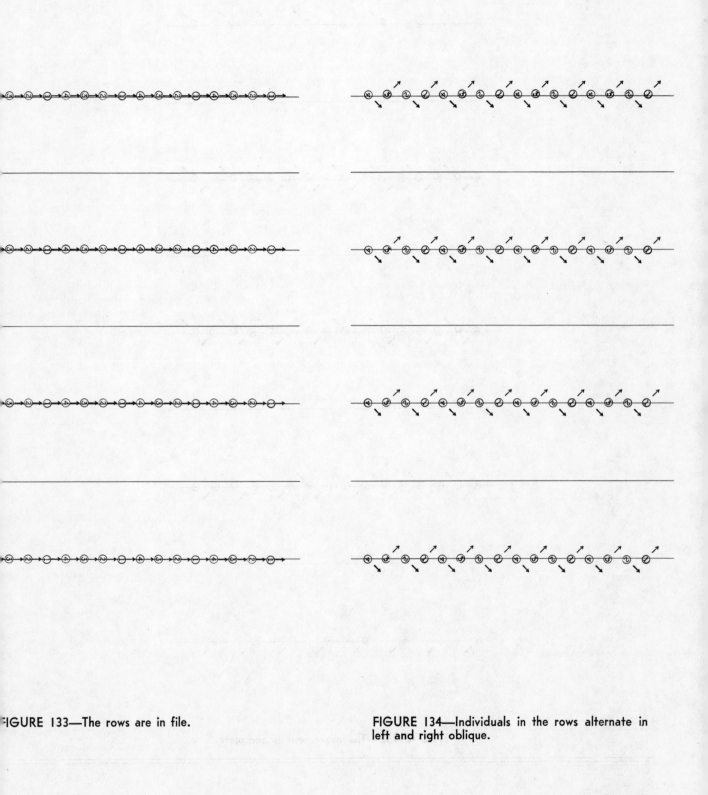

FIGURE 133—The rows are in file.

FIGURE 134—Individuals in the rows alternate in left and right oblique.

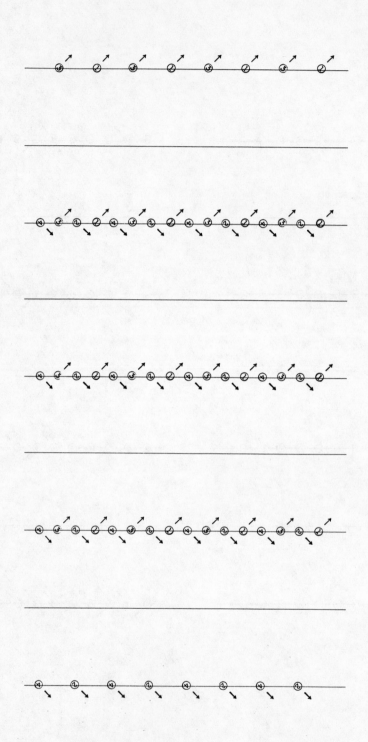

FIGURE 135—The movement is complete.

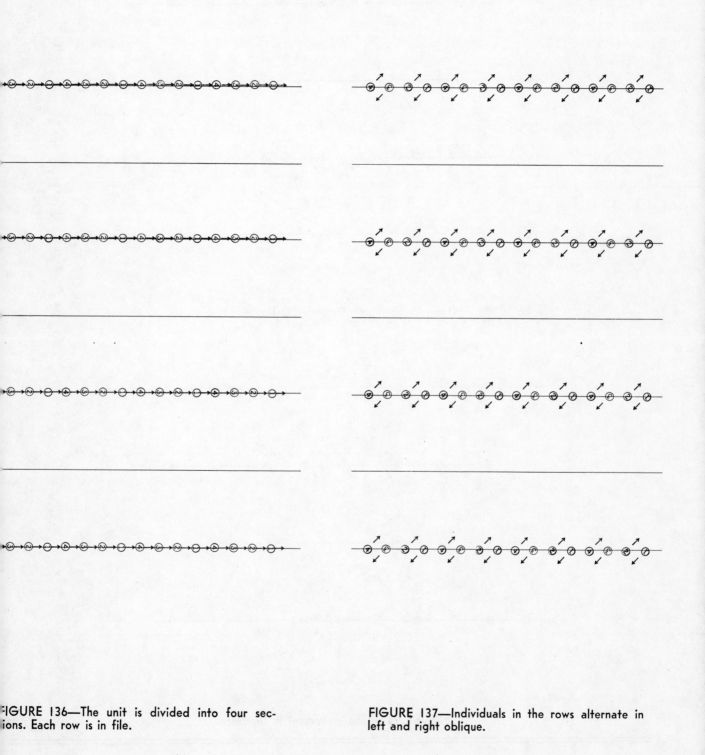

FIGURE 136—The unit is divided into four sections. Each row is in file.

FIGURE 137—Individuals in the rows alternate in left and right oblique.

FIGURE 138—The movement is complete.

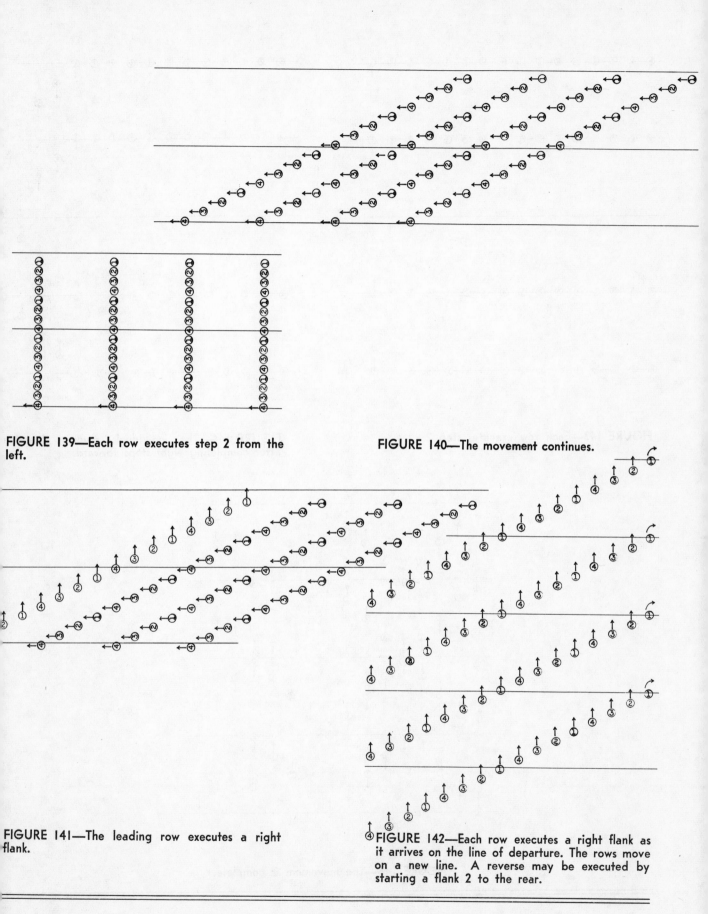

FIGURE 139—Each row executes step 2 from the left.

FIGURE 140—The movement continues.

FIGURE 141—The leading row executes a right flank.

FIGURE 142—Each row executes a right flank as it arrives on the line of departure. The rows move on a new line. A reverse may be executed by starting a flank 2 to the rear.

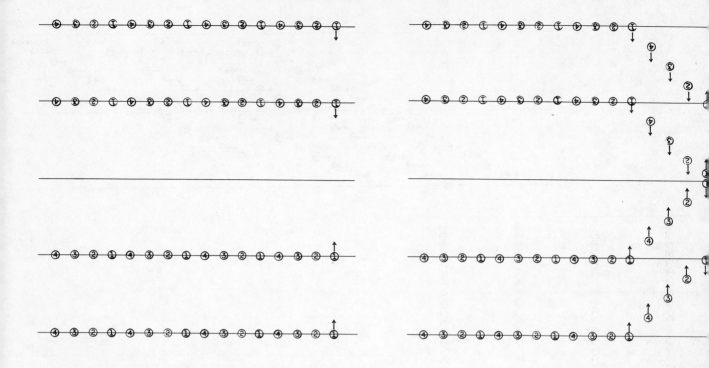

FIGURE 143—Each row executes step 2.

FIGURE 144—The individuals reverse direction after completing eight steps forward.

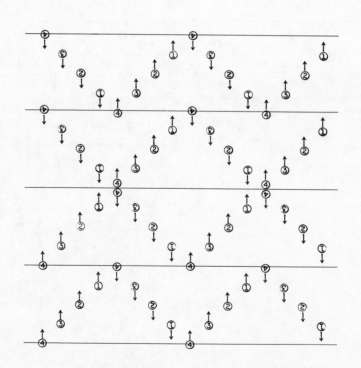

FIGURE 145—The movement is complete.

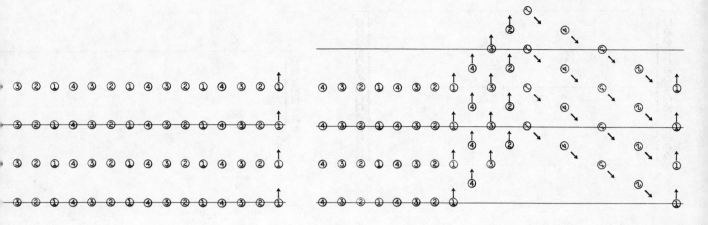

FIGURE 146—Each row executes step 2.

FIGURE 147—Each individual moves forward a definite number of steps and turns to the right 135 degrees, moves a definite number of steps and turns to the left 135 degrees to resume forward motion.

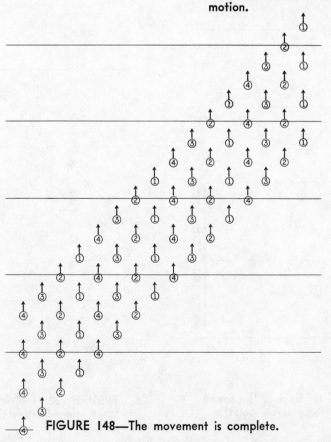

FIGURE 148—The movement is complete.

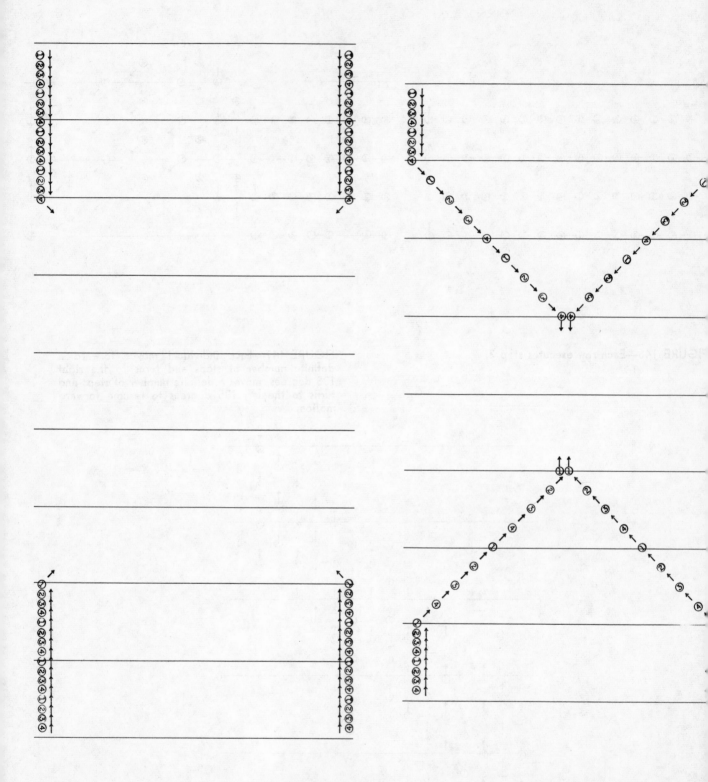

FIGURE 149—Each row executes flank 2. The rows execute a side step to allow for a single point of departure for each row.

FIGURE 150—Individuals execute turns as they meet opposite rows. The drill may be continued in file.

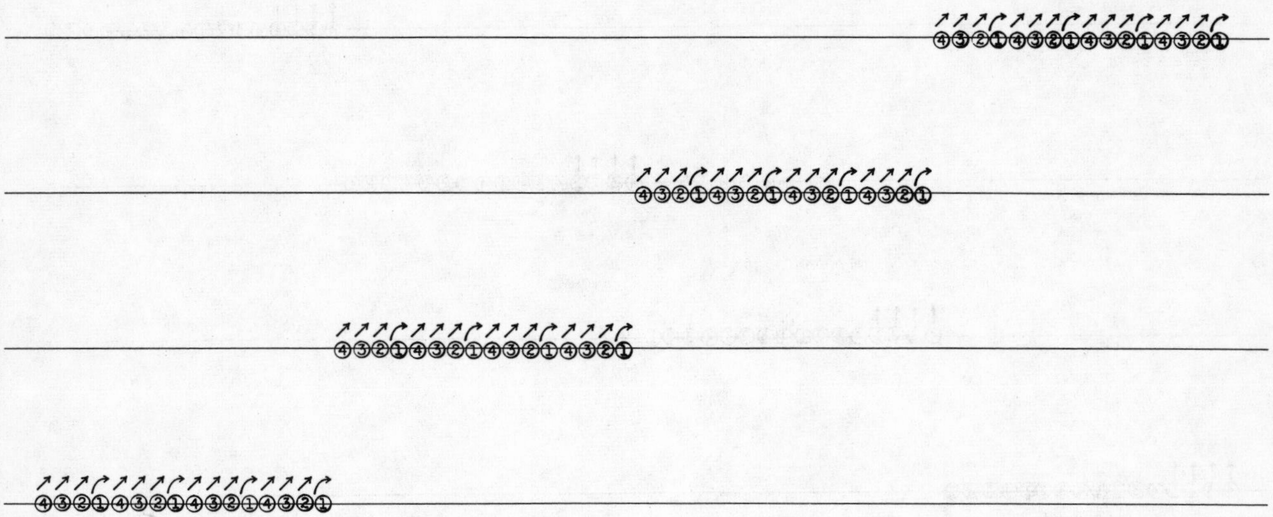

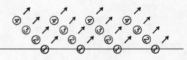

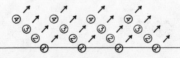

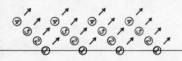

FIGURE 151—The unit is in staggered formation. Each squad executes squad half right and moves in the new direction.

FIGURE 152—The movement is complete.

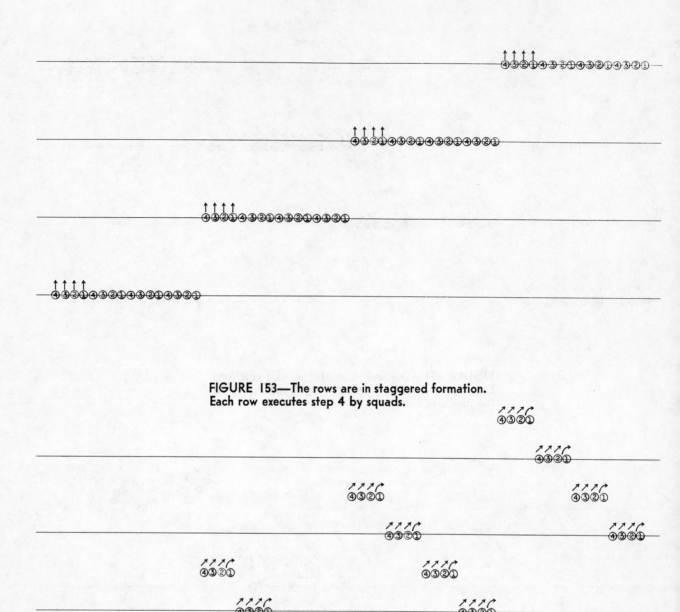

FIGURE 153—The rows are in staggered formation. Each row executes step 4 by squads.

FIGURE 154—Each squad executes a squad half right and step 2 from the left. The members of the squad side step to allow for a single point of departure for each squad.

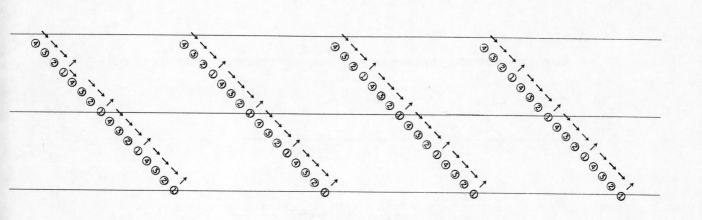

FIGURE 155—The movement continues.

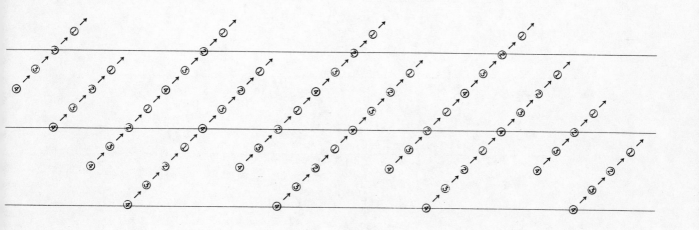

FIGURE 156—The movement is complete.

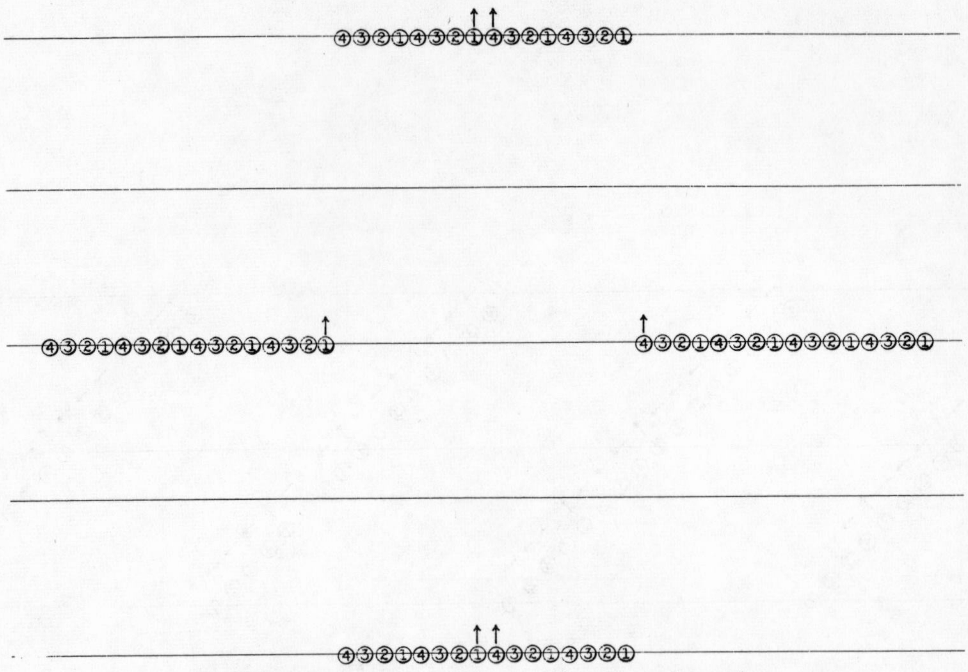

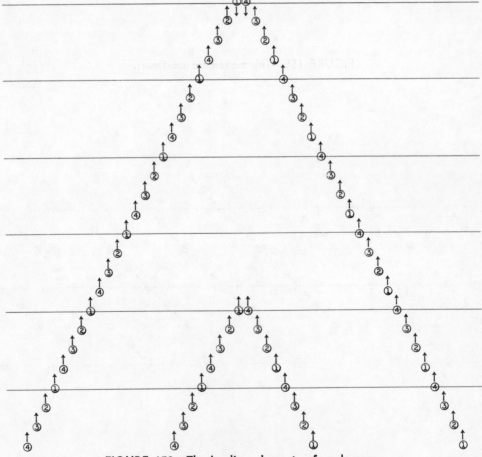

FIGURE 157—Two rows execute step 2 from the center. Two rows execute step 2 from the flanks.

FIGURE 158—The leading elements of each arrow head can change direction for a definite number of steps.

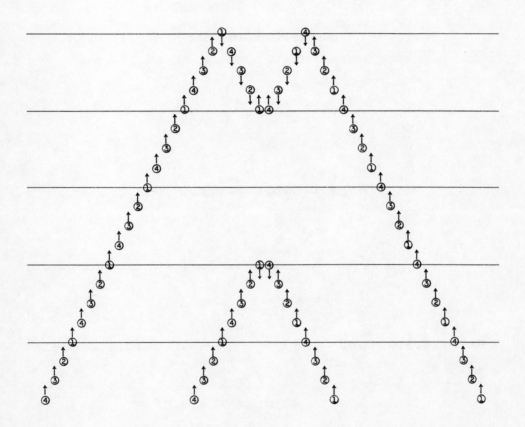

FIGURE 159—The movement continues.

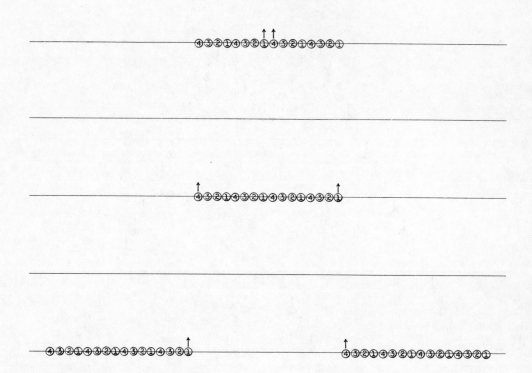

FIGURE 160—The rows execute step 2.

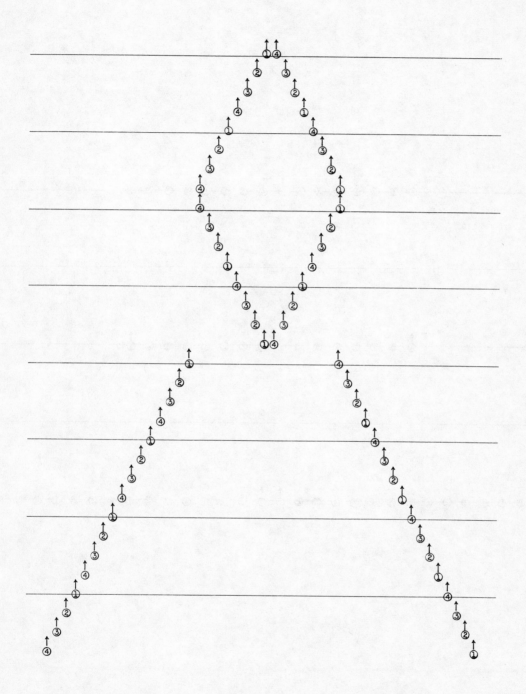

FIGURE 161—The movement is complete. The unit is in position for file drills.

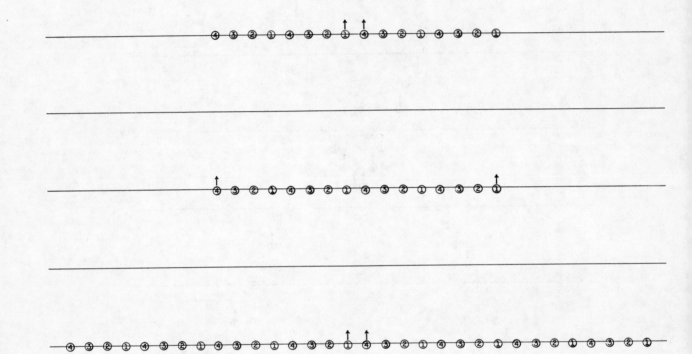

FIGURE 162—Each row executes step 2.

FIGURE 163—The movement is complete. The unit
is in position for file drills.

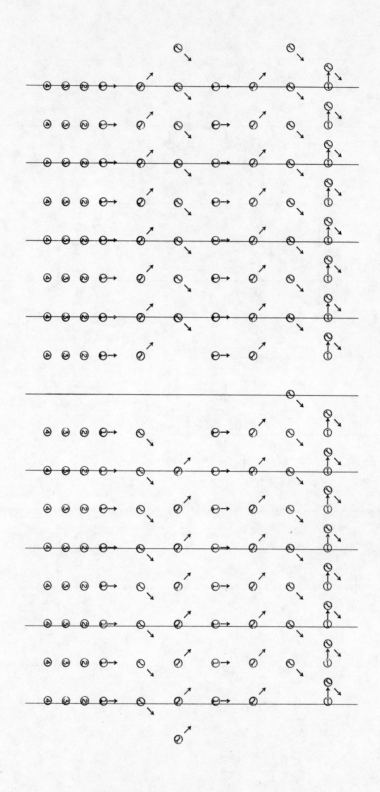

FIGURE 164—Each squad is in file. The number ones represent a suggested turn to be followed by squad file.

The Squares

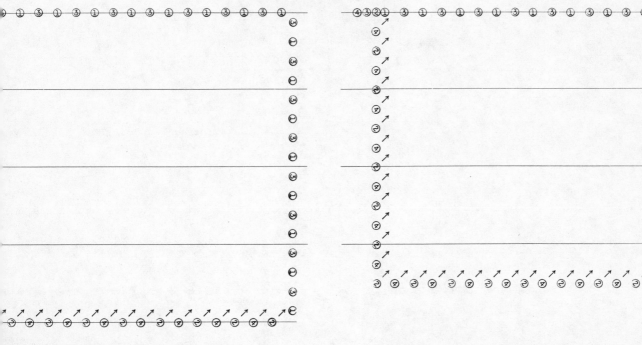

FIGURE 165—Two sides of the square oblique to close with the two adjacent sides.

FIGURE 166—The movement continues.

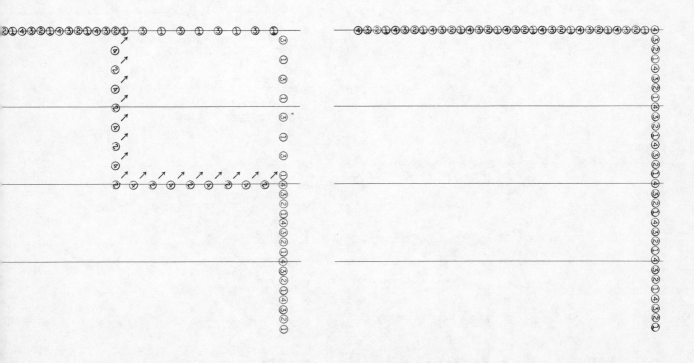

FIGURE 167—The movement continues.

FIGURE 168—The movement is complete.

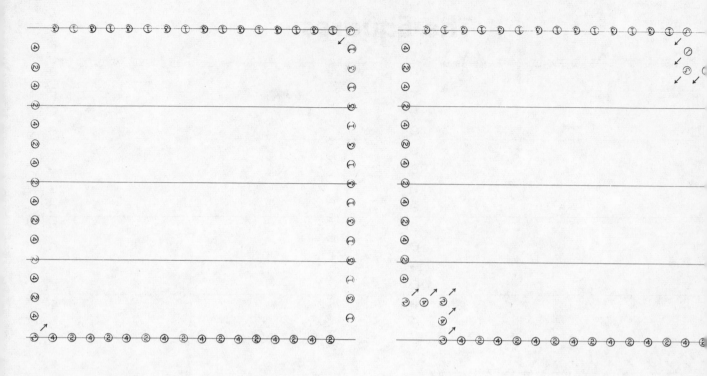

FIGURE 169—Opposite corners oblique toward the center.

FIGURE 170—The movement continues.

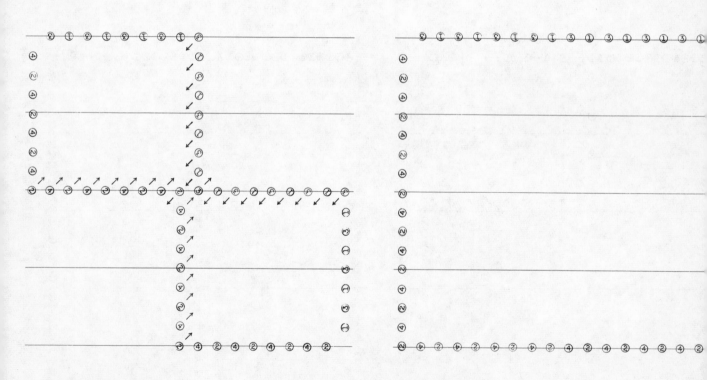

FIGURE 171—Individuals execute to-the-rear as they reach the diagonal.

FIGURE 172—The movement is complete.

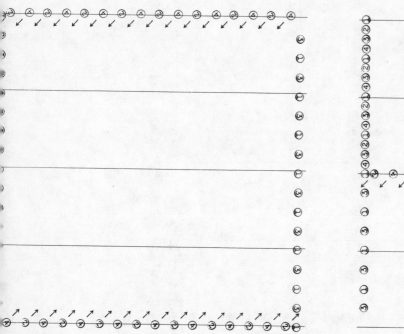

FIGURE 173—Two sides oblique on to line.

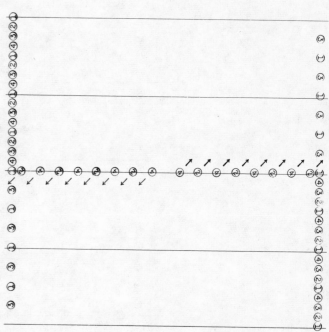

FIGURE 174—The movement continues.

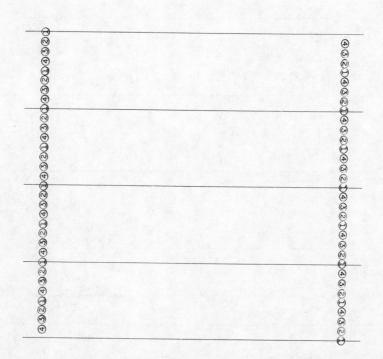

FIGURE 175—The movement is complete.

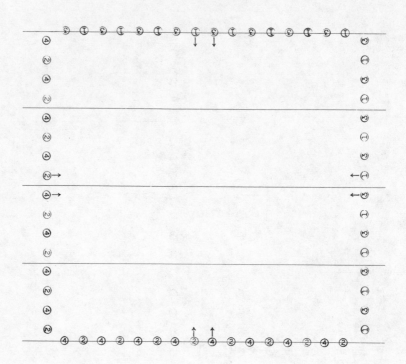

FIGURE 176—Each side executes step 2 from the center.

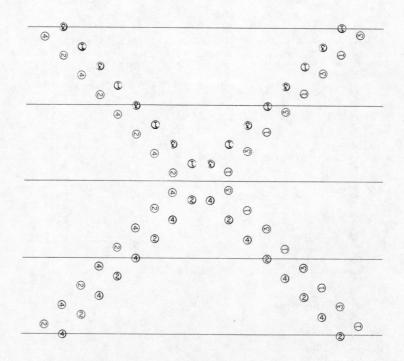

FIGURE 177—The movement is complete. The unit is in position for pattern drill or reverse the movement.

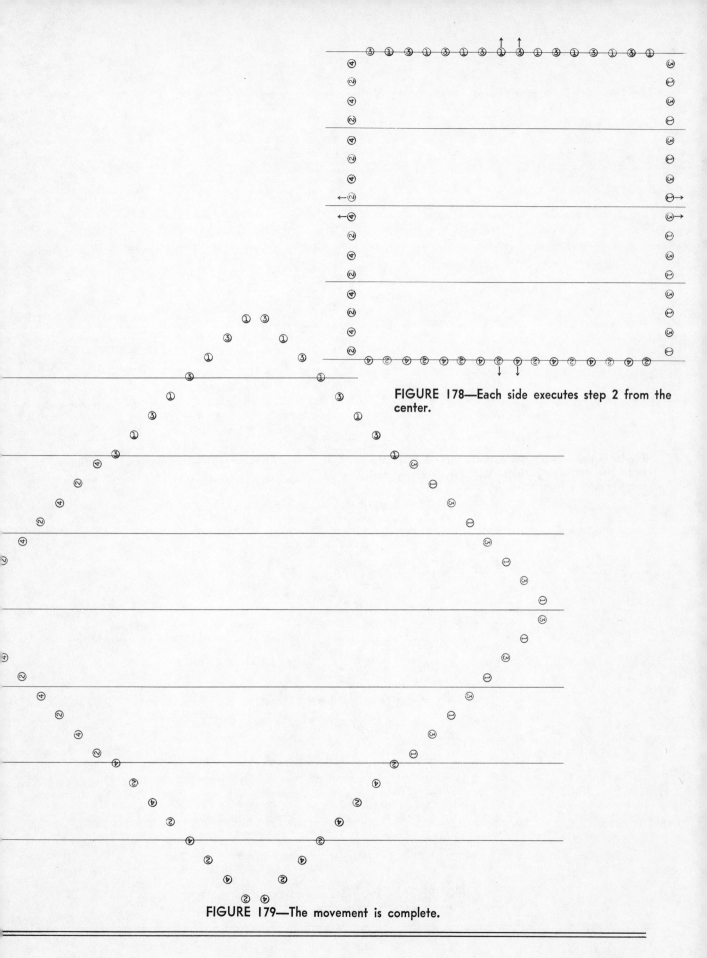

FIGURE 178—Each side executes step 2 from the center.

FIGURE 179—The movement is complete.

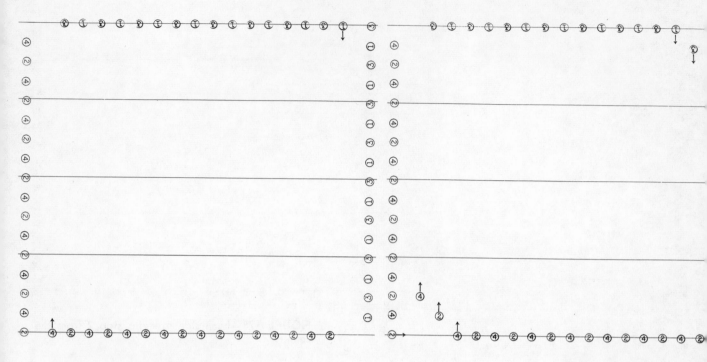

FIGURE 180—Two sides execute step 2 from the left. The remaining sides hold for 4 steps and execute step 2 from the right.

FIGURE 181—The movement continues.

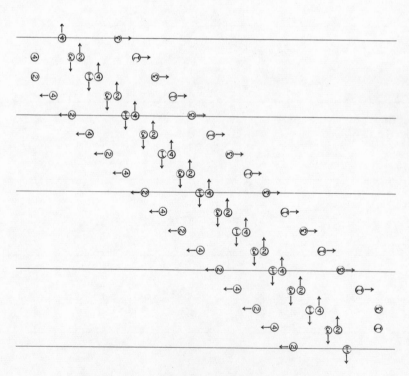

FIGURE 182—Two sides move through each other. The remaining sides reverse direction.

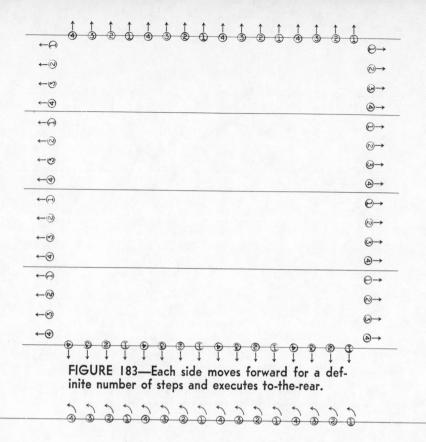

FIGURE 183—Each side moves forward for a definite number of steps and executes to-the-rear.

FIGURE 184—The movement continues.

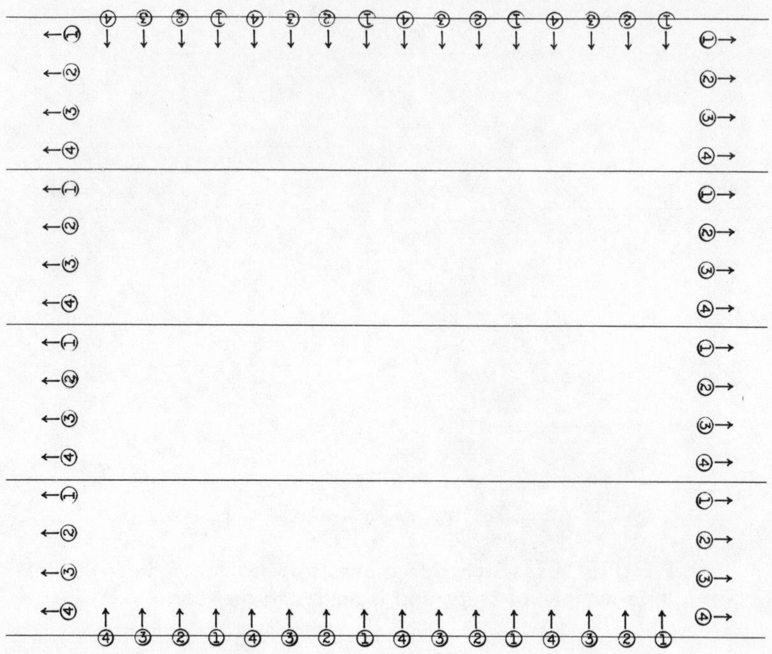

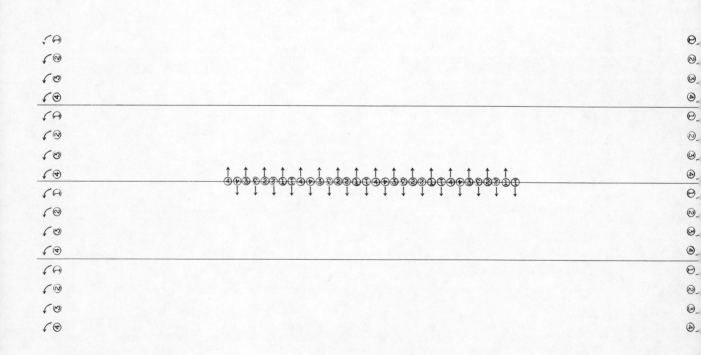

FIGURE 185—Two sides move toward the center, mesh and continue to the opposite side. The other sides move out for 16 steps and execute to-the-rear.

FIGURE 186—The movement continues.

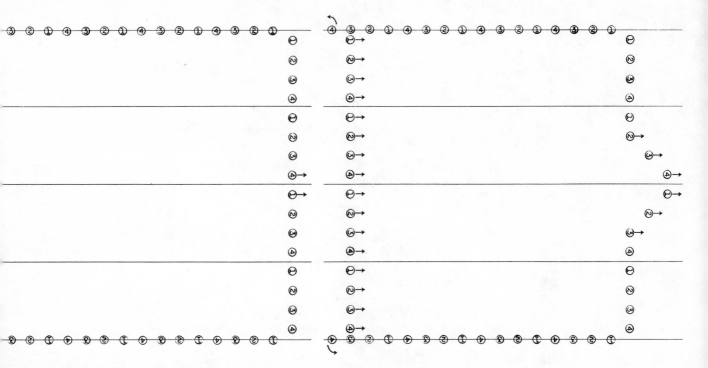

FIGURE 187—One side executes step 2 from the center. The opposite side moves forward. The remaining sides execute step 2 from one end after a four step hold.

FIGURE 188—The movement continues.

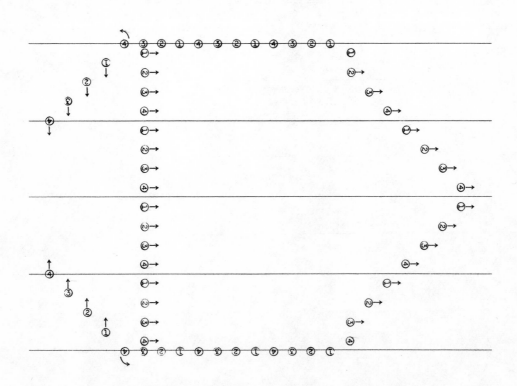

FIGURE 189—The movement continues.

FIGURE 190—The corners move out at an oblique for a definite number of steps and execute to-the-rear.

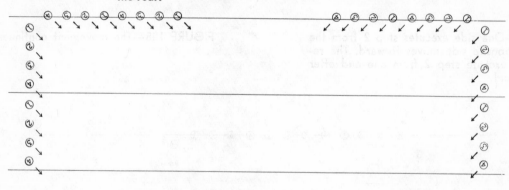

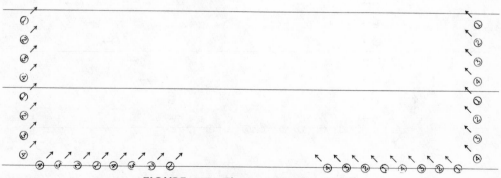

FIGURE 191—The movement continues.

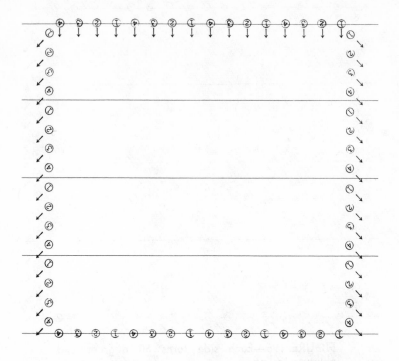

FIGURE 192—One side moves forward and meshes with the opposite side. The remaining sides oblique (60 degree turn) on to line.

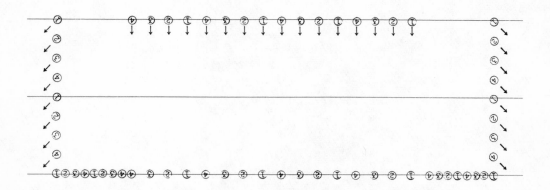

FIGURE 193—The movement continues.

FIGURE 194—The movement continues.

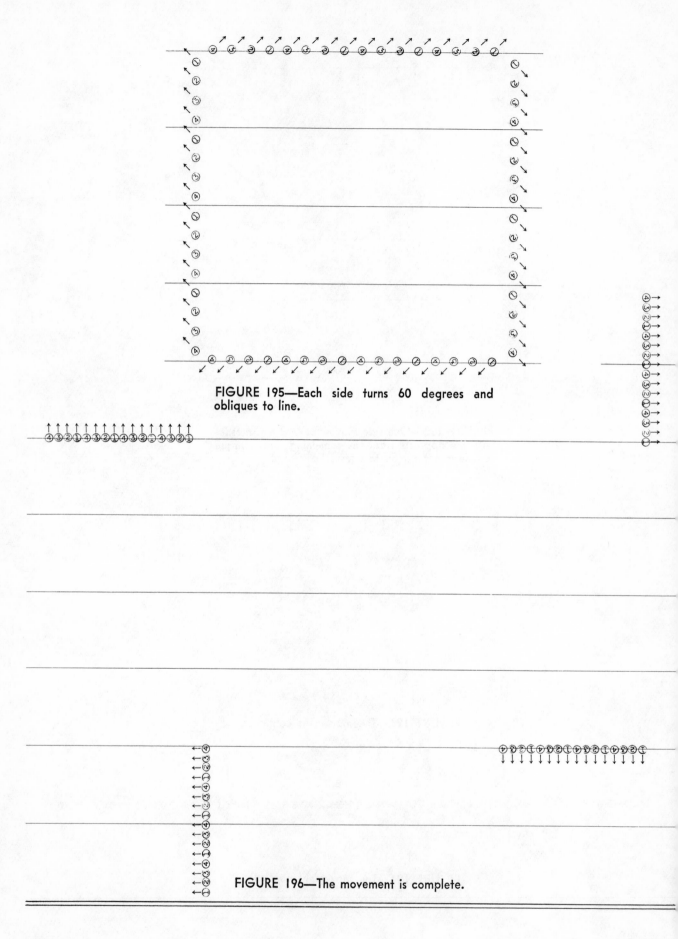

FIGURE 195—Each side turns 60 degrees and obliques to line.

FIGURE 196—The movement is complete.

FIGURE 197—Each side turns 60 degrees to the right and obliques on to line.

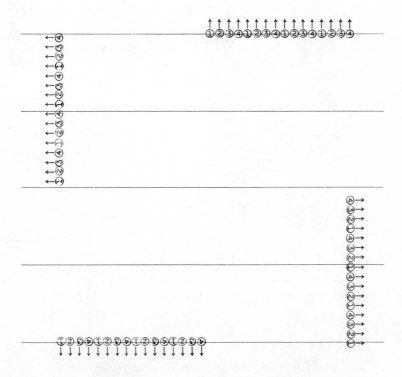

FIGURE 198—The movement is complete.

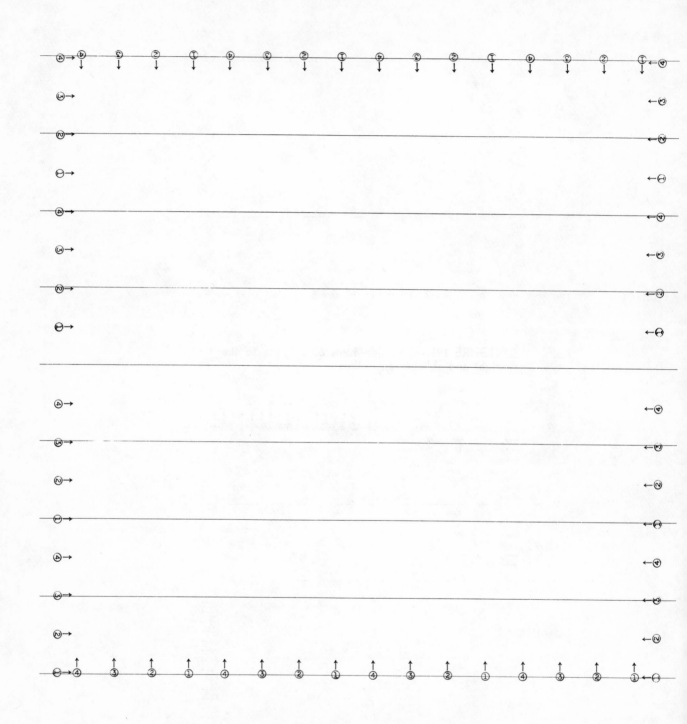

FIGURE 199—Each side moves forward toward the
center. Adjacent sides are moving at 2 step offset.

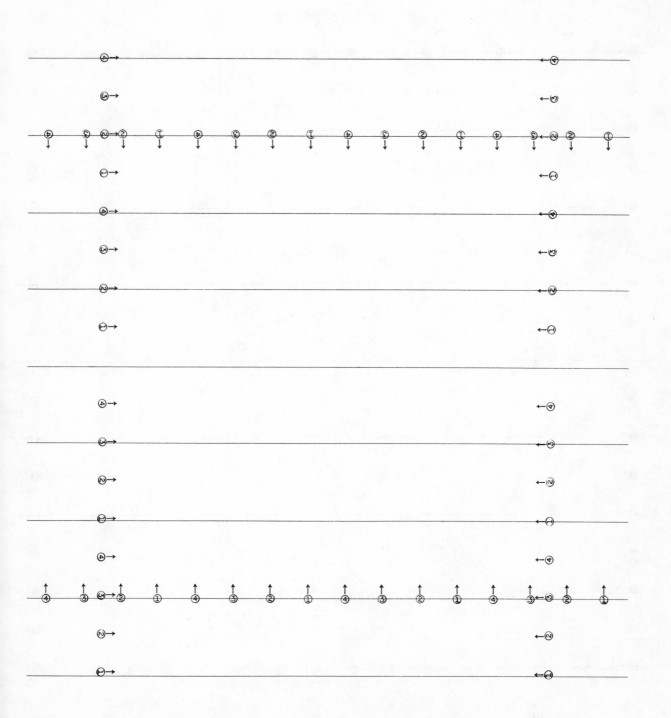

FIGURE 200—The movement continues.

FIGURE 201—Each side executes step 2 from both
flanks. Adjacent sides are at 2 step offset.

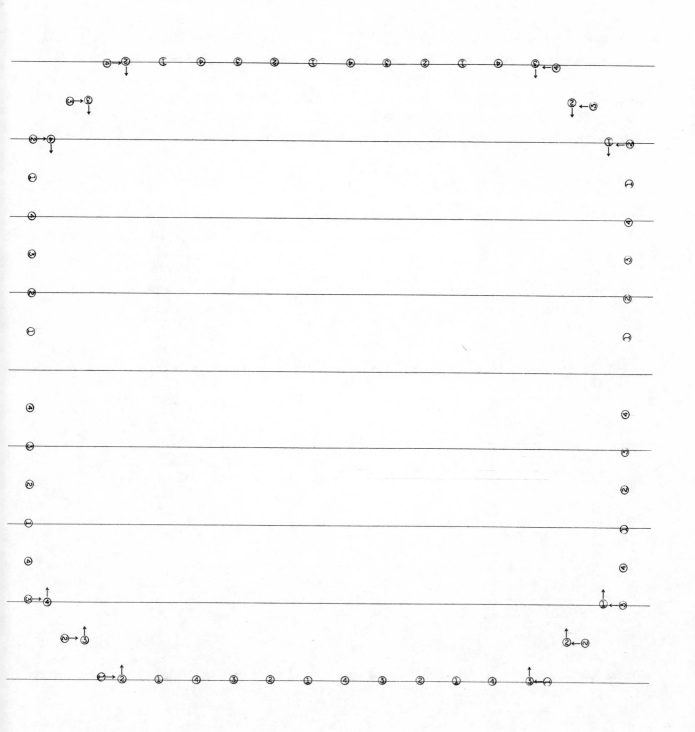

FIGURE 202—The movement continues.

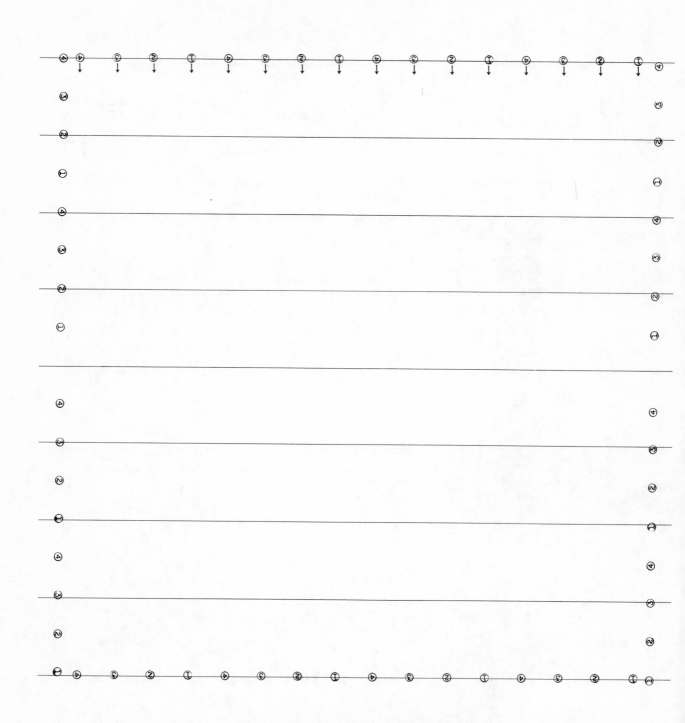

FIGURE 203—Each side moves forward. A definite number of steps space the individual sides. The forward direction can be toward the inside or toward the outside.

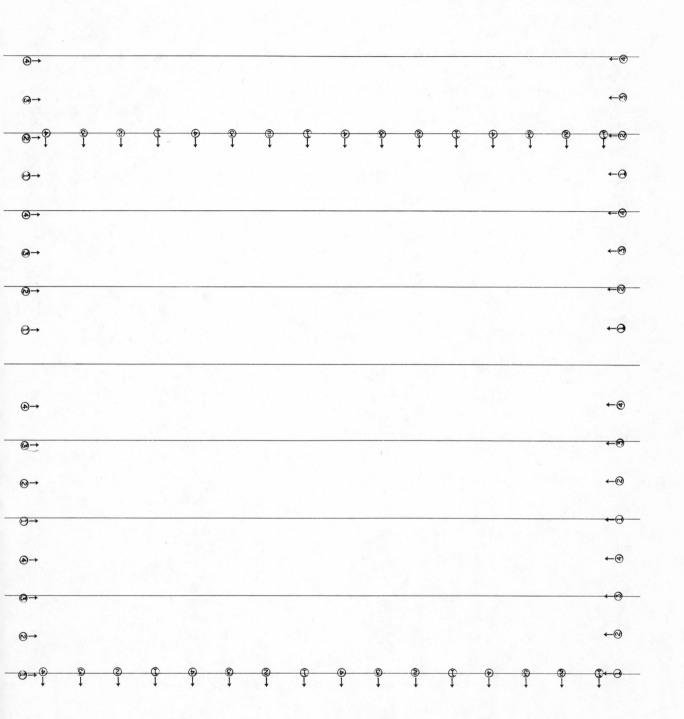

FIGURE 204—The movement continues.

FIGURE 205—Each side moves at oblique. The
adjacent sides are at 2 step offset.

FIGURE 206—The movement continues.

FIGURE 207—Each side moves at an oblique. Individuals hold as they arrive on the diagonal line.

FIGURE 208—The movement is complete.

FIGURE 209—Two sides move forward.

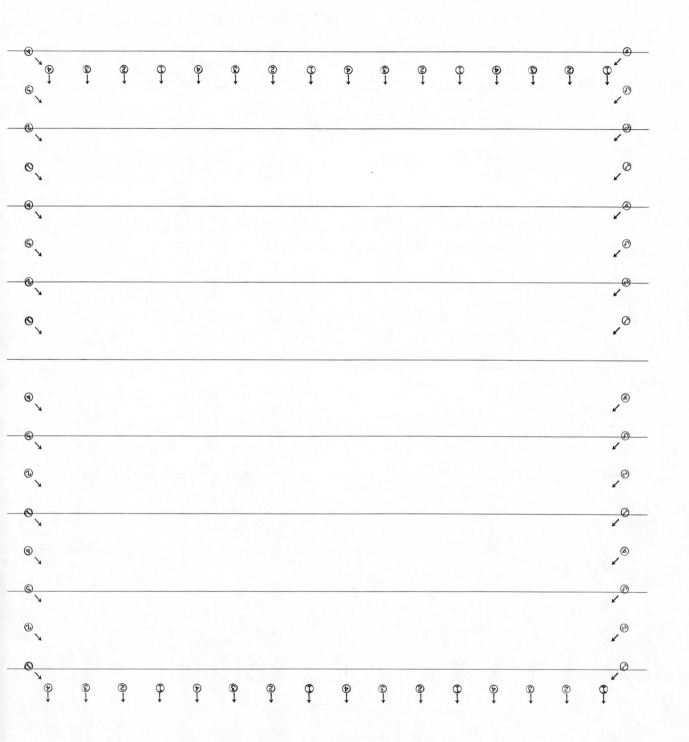

FIGURE 210—The remaining sides move out at an oblique.

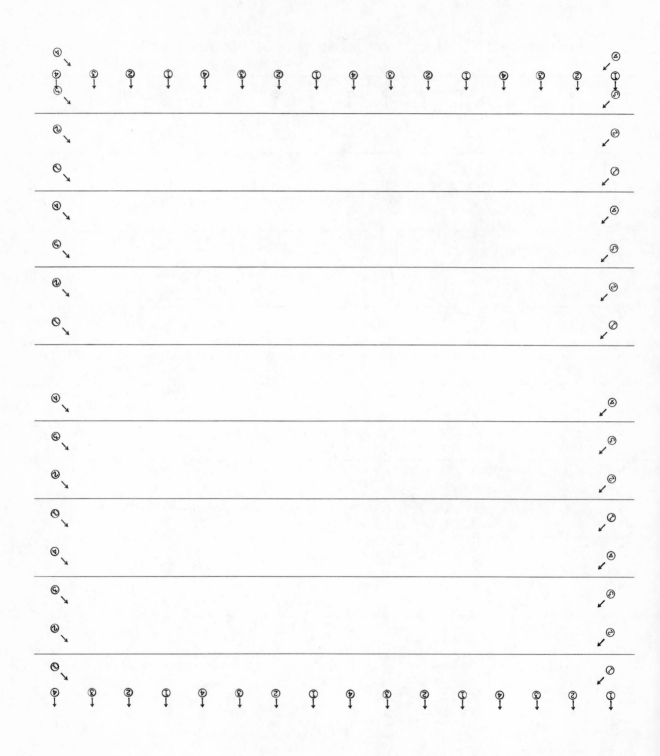

FIGURE 211—The movement continues.

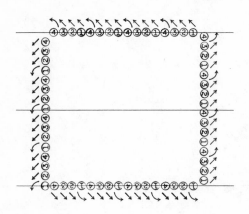

FIGURE 212—Each squad executes squad right and forward.

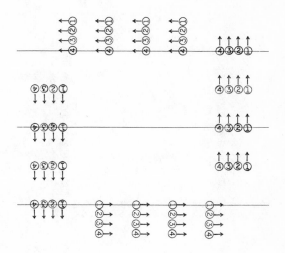

FIGURE 213—The movement continues.

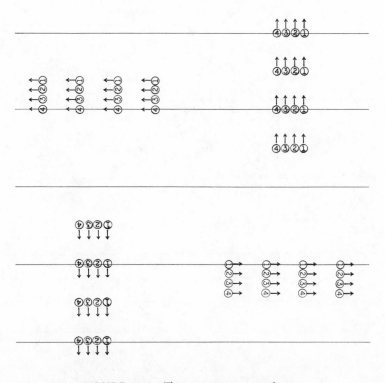

FIGURE 214—The movement continues.

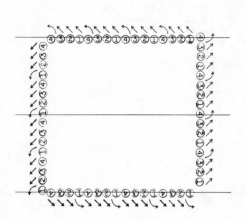

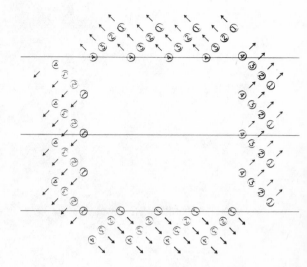

FIGURE 215—Each squad executes squad half left and forward.

FIGURE 216—The movement continues.

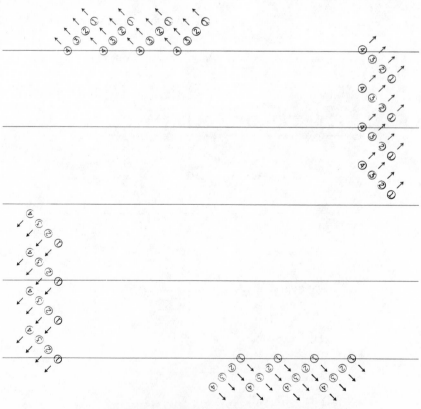

FIGURE 217—The movement continues.

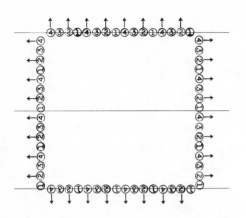

FIGURE 218—Twos and fours move forward. The ones and threes hold for a definite number of steps.

FIGURE 219—The movement continues.

FIGURE 220—The twos and fours execute to-the-rear.

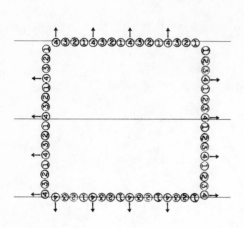

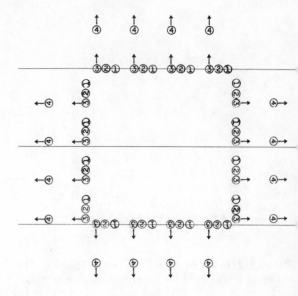

FIGURE 221—Each squad executes step four. The squad members shift to keep a point of departure.

FIGURE 222—The movement continues.

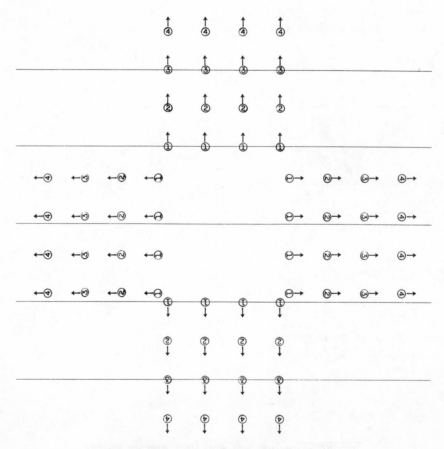

FIGURE 223—The movement is complete.

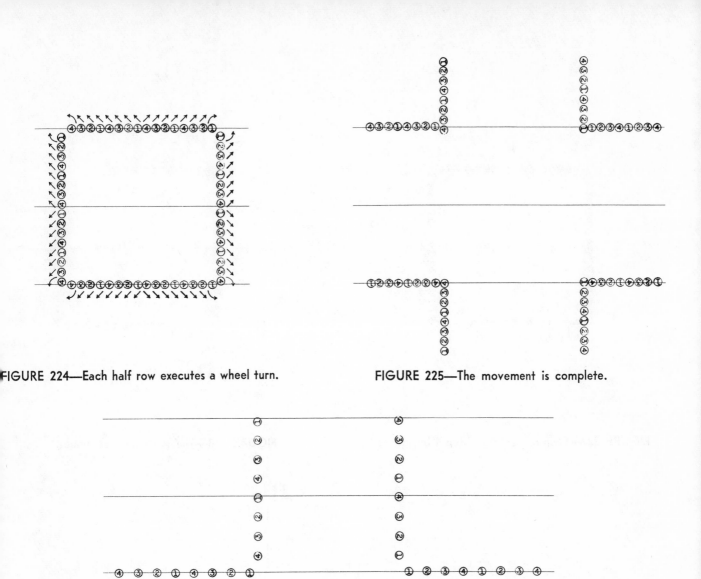

FIGURE 224—Each half row executes a wheel turn.

FIGURE 225—The movement is complete.

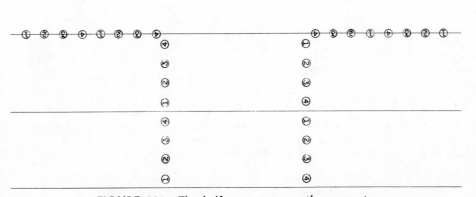

FIGURE 226—The half rows open as they execute
the wheel turn.

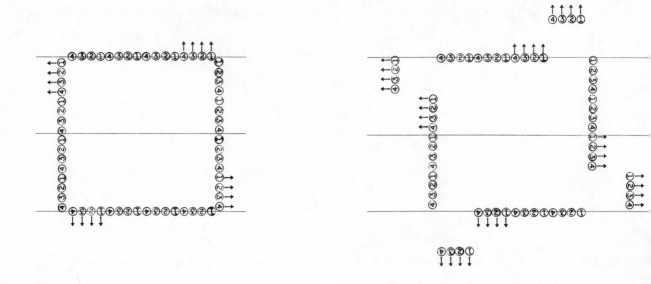

FIGURE 227—Each row executes step 4 by squads.　　　　FIGURE 228—The movement continues.

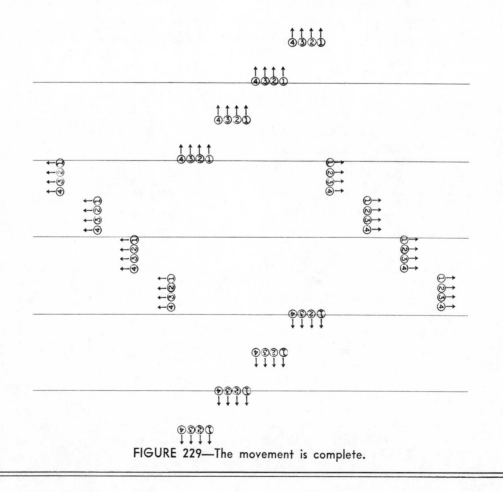

FIGURE 229—The movement is complete.

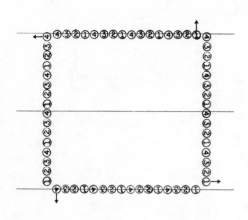

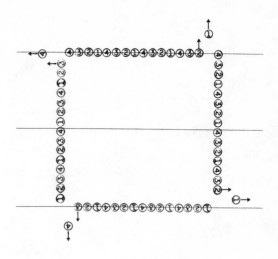

FIGURE 230—Each row executes step 2 from the right.

FIGURE 231—The movement continues.

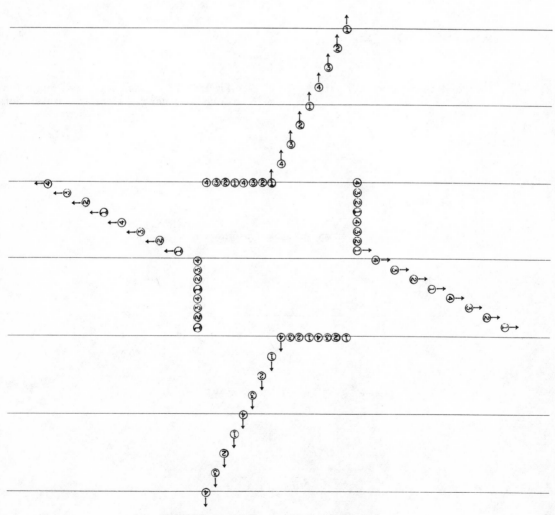

FIGURE 232—The movement continues.

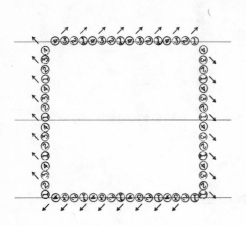

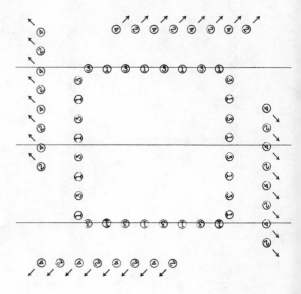

FIGURE 233—The twos and fours execute right oblique.

FIGURE 234—The ones and threes hold for a definite number of steps and execute left oblique.

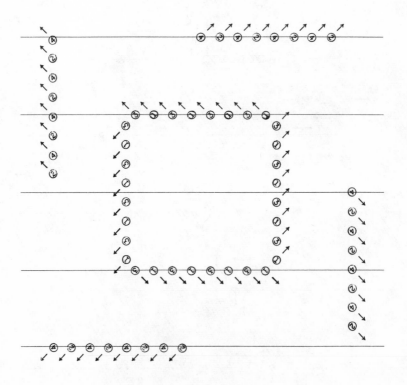

FIGURE 235—The movement is complete.

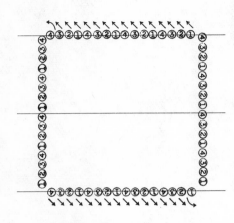

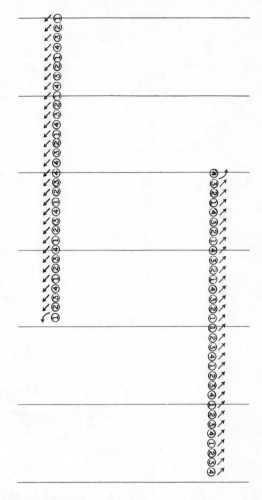

FIGURE 236—Two sides execute wheel turns to the left.

FIGURE 237—Two sides in line execute a wheel turn to the left.

FIGURE 238—Each side executes a wheel turn to the left.

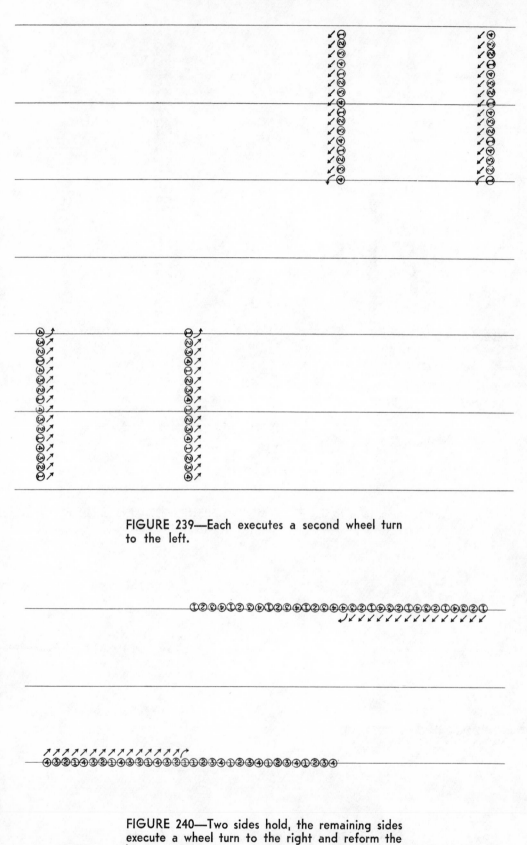

FIGURE 239—Each executes a second wheel turn to the left.

FIGURE 240—Two sides hold, the remaining sides execute a wheel turn to the right and reform the box.

The "L"

FIGURE 241—The unit executes step 2 from the corner.

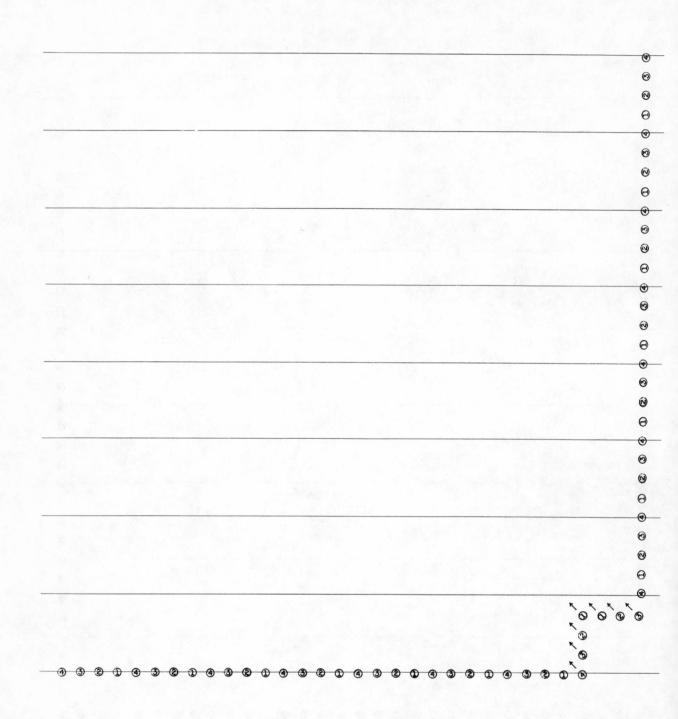

FIGURE 242—The movement continues.

FIGURE 243—The movement is complete.

FIGURE 244—Each side executes step 2.

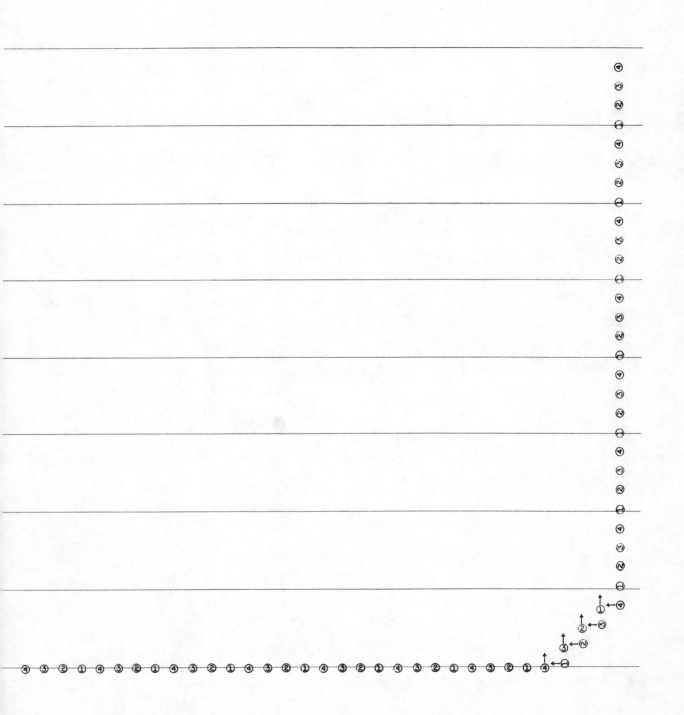

FIGURE 245—The movement continues.

FIGURE 246—The movement is complete.

FIGURE 247—Each side executes step 2.

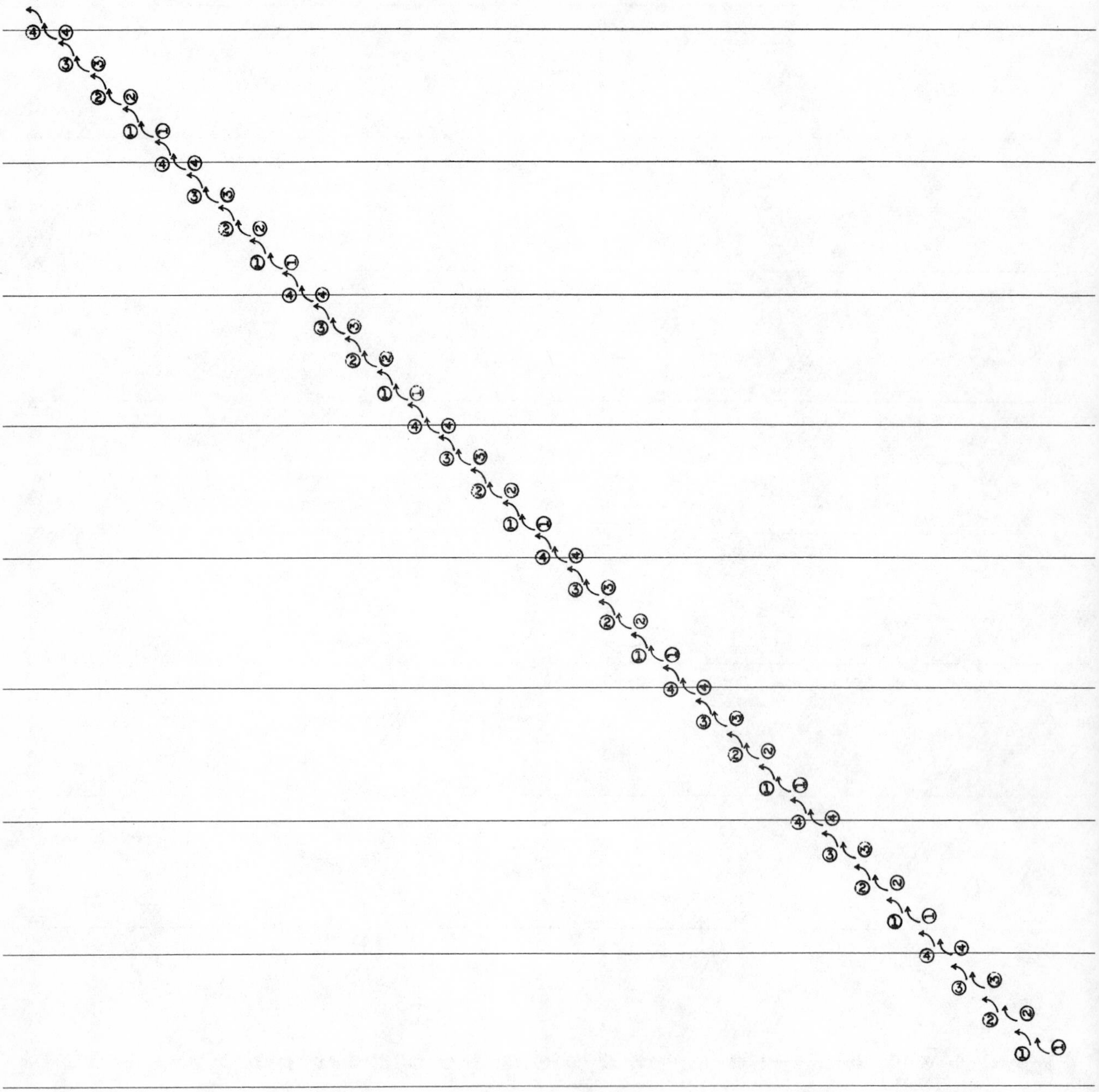

FIGURE 248—Both sides execute a turn and move
on to a new line.

FIGURE 249—The movement is complete.

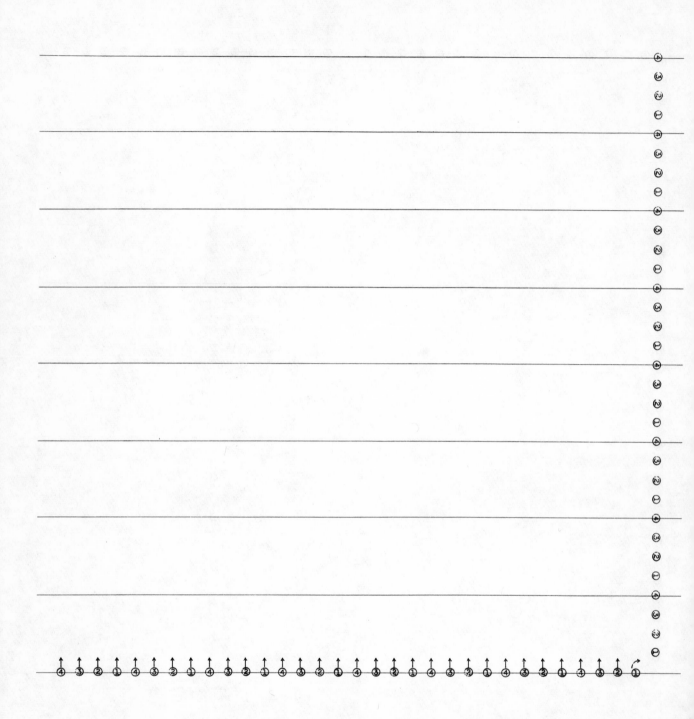

FIGURE 250—One side executes flank 2 and moves on line.

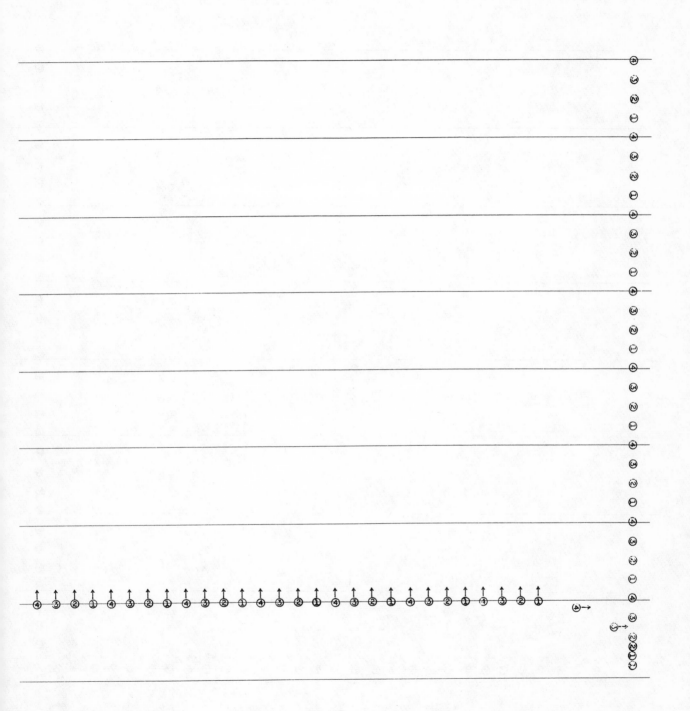

FIGURE 251—The movement continues.

FIGURE 252—One side obliques and moves on line.

FIGURE 253—The remaining side holds for 4 steps
and executes step 2.

FIGURE 254—Each side executes step 2.

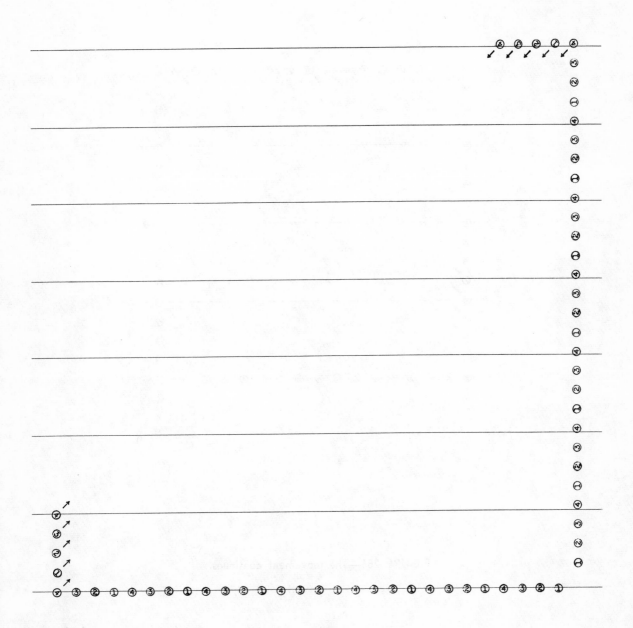

FIGURE 255—The movement continues.

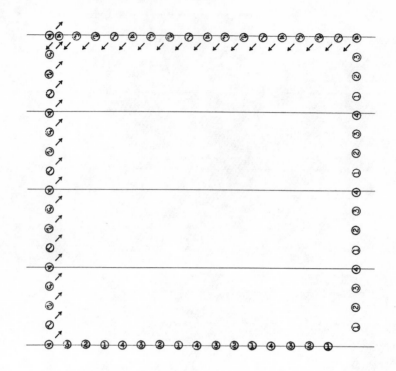

FIGURE 256—The movement continues.

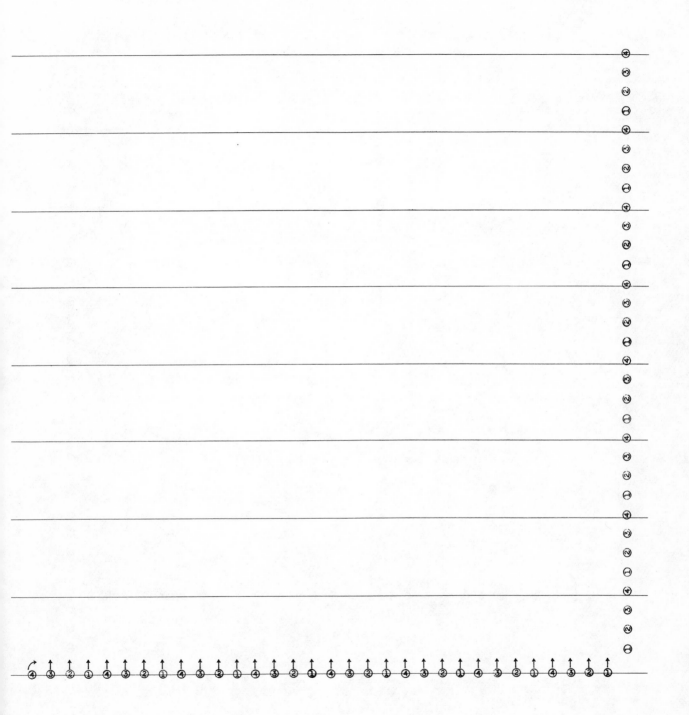

FIGURE 257—One side moves forward and executes flank 2 followed by half step.

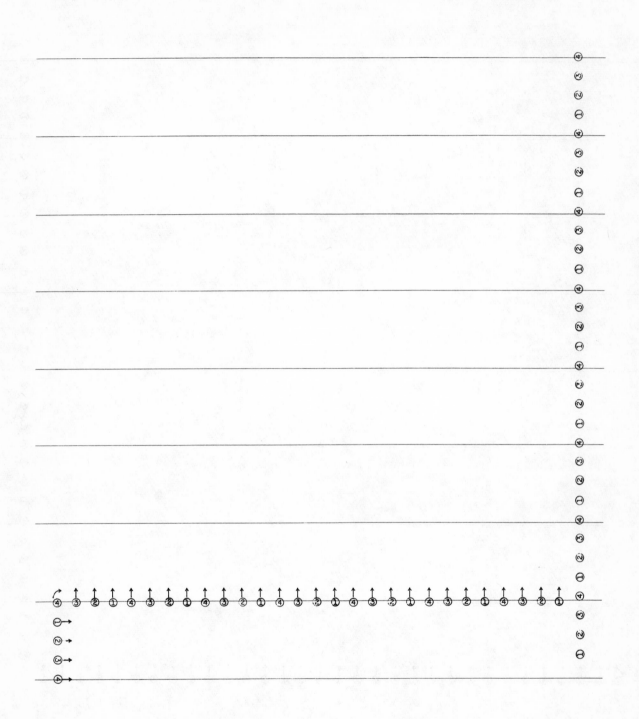

FIGURE 258—The movement continues.

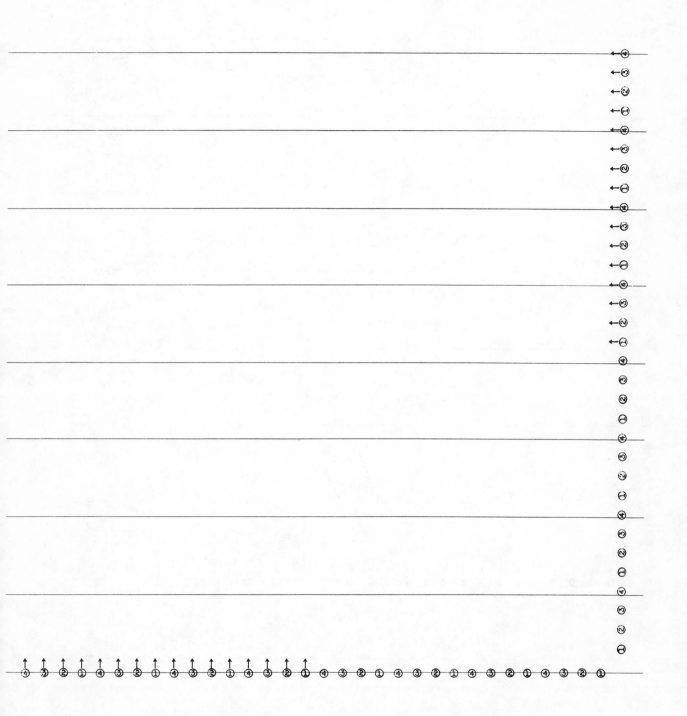

FIGURE 259—One half of each side moves forward, the remaining halves hold for a definite number of steps.

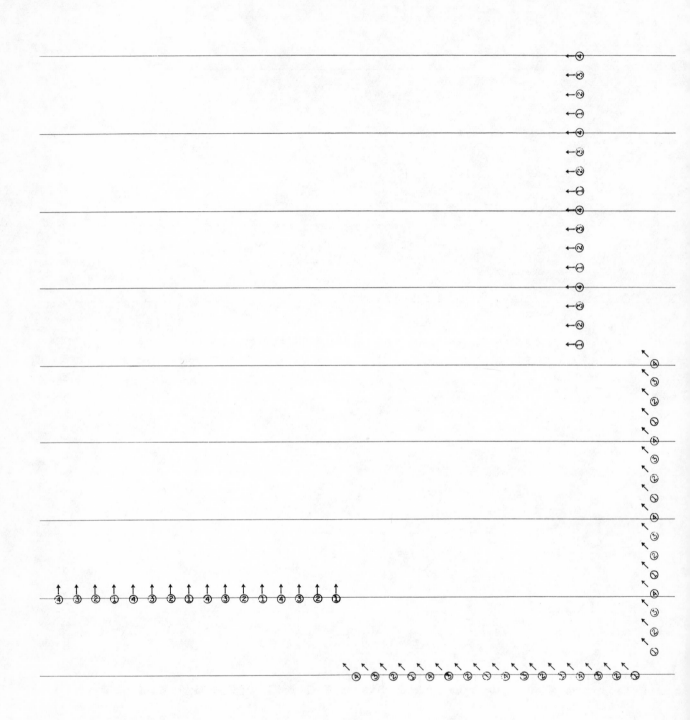

FIGURE 260—The movement continues with forward and oblique motion.

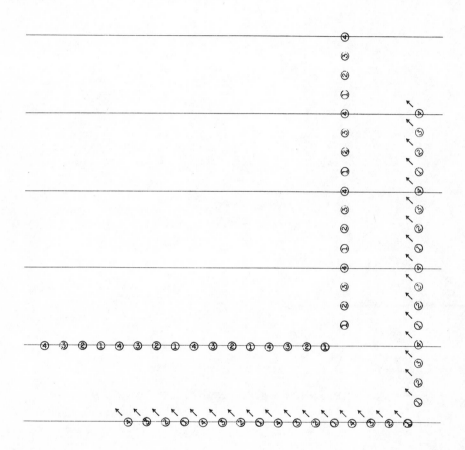

FIGURE 261—The movement continues.

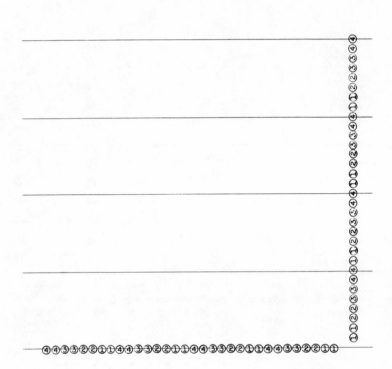

FIGURE 262—The movement is complete.

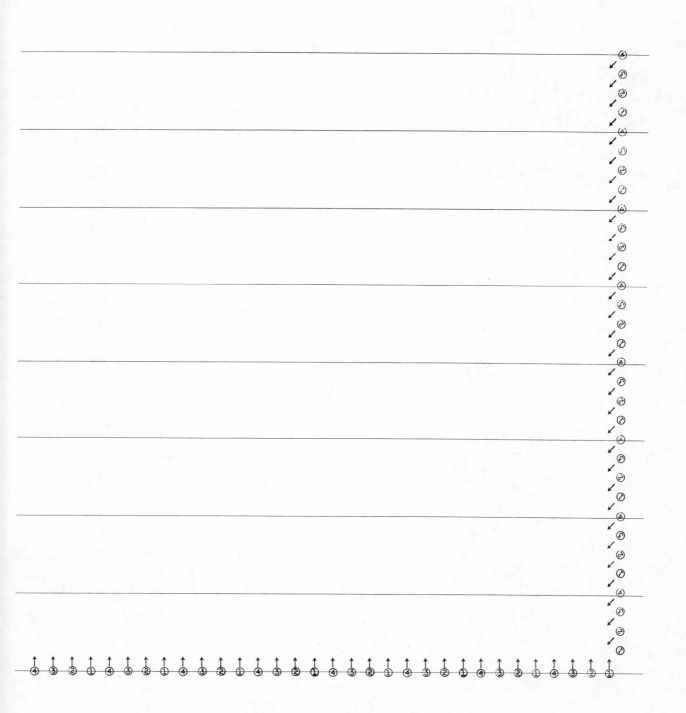

FIGURE 263—One side moves forward, the other side moves at oblique.

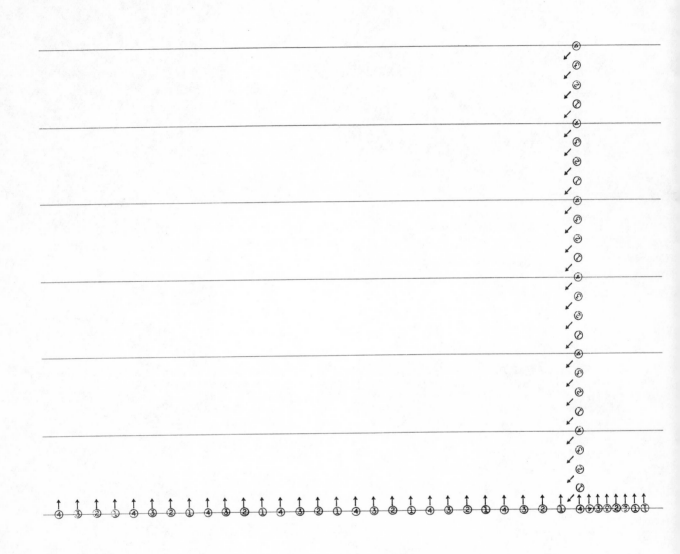

FIGURE 264—The obliquing side is picked up as the
lines mesh.

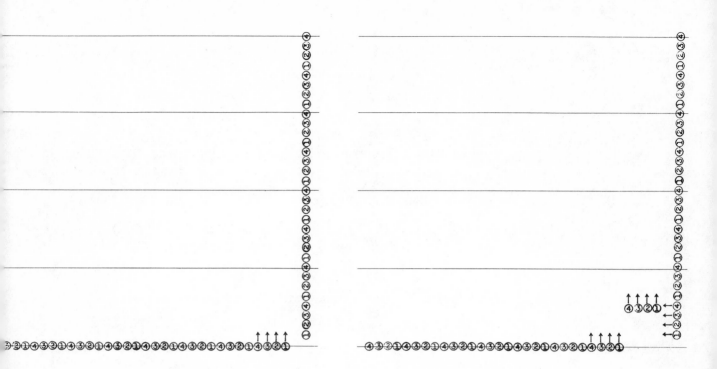

FIGURE 265—Each side executes step 4 by squads. One side holds for a definite number of steps before starting the execution.

FIGURE 266—The movement continues.

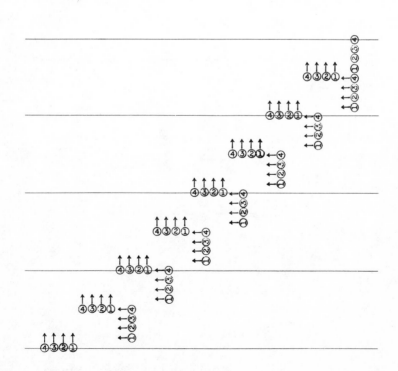

FIGURE 267—The movement continues.

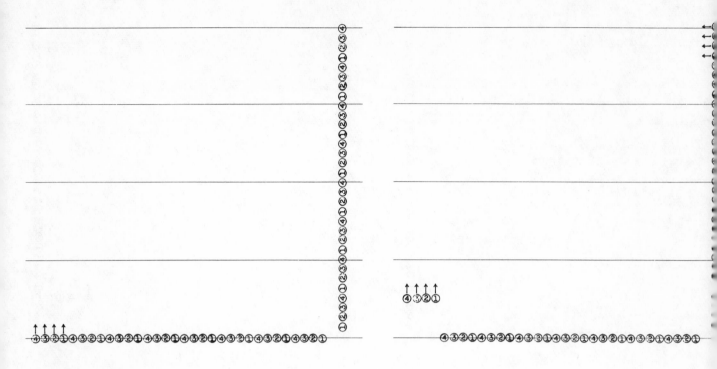

FIGURE 268—Each side executes step 8 by squads. One side holds for 4 steps before starting the execution.

FIGURE 269—The movement continues.

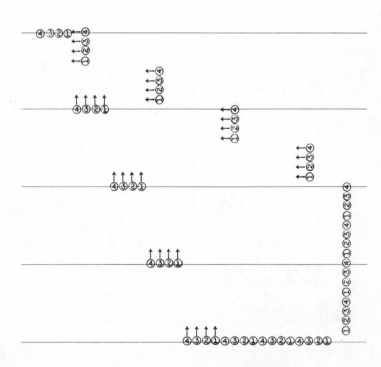

FIGURE 270—The movement continues.

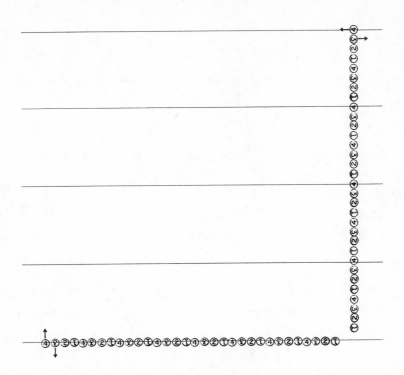

FIGURE 271—Each meshed side executes step 2.

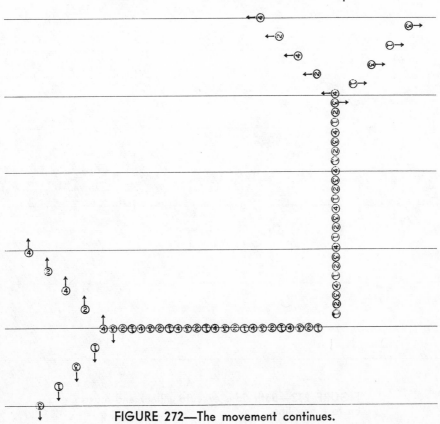

FIGURE 272—The movement continues.

FIGURE 273—Both sides execute a flank and move on to a new line.

FIGURE 274—The movement is complete.

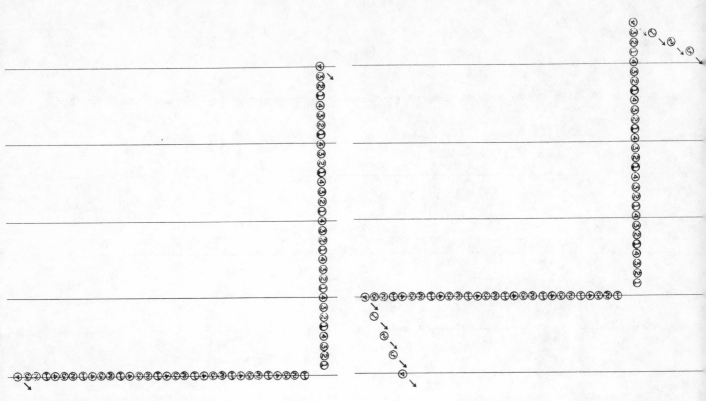

FIGURE 275—Each side executes step 2 and obliques on to new line.

FIGURE 276—The movement continues.

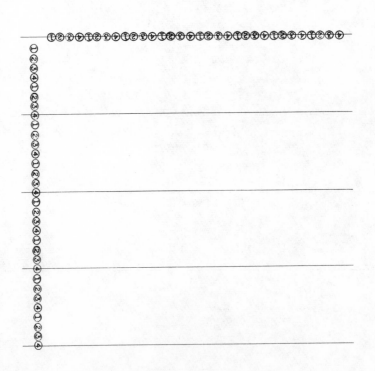

FIGURE 277—The movement is complete.

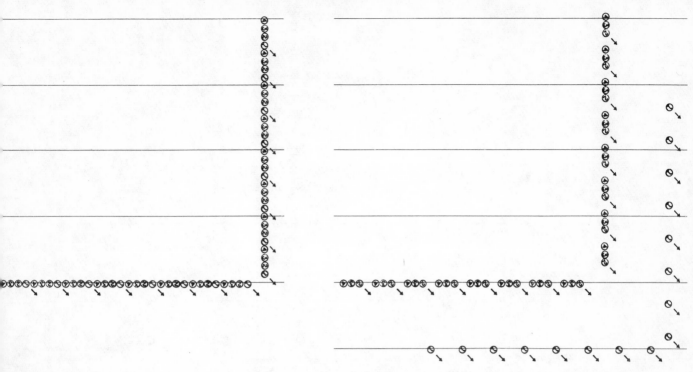

FIGURE 278—Each squad executes step 8 and moves in an oblique.

FIGURE 279—The movement continues.

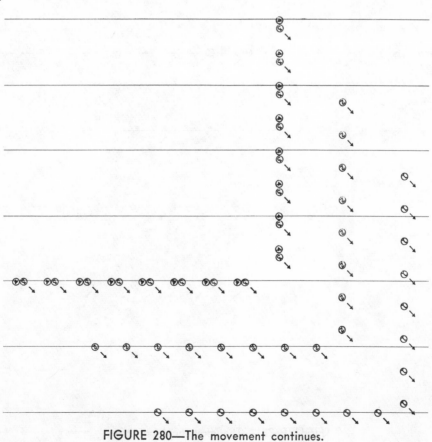

FIGURE 280—The movement continues.

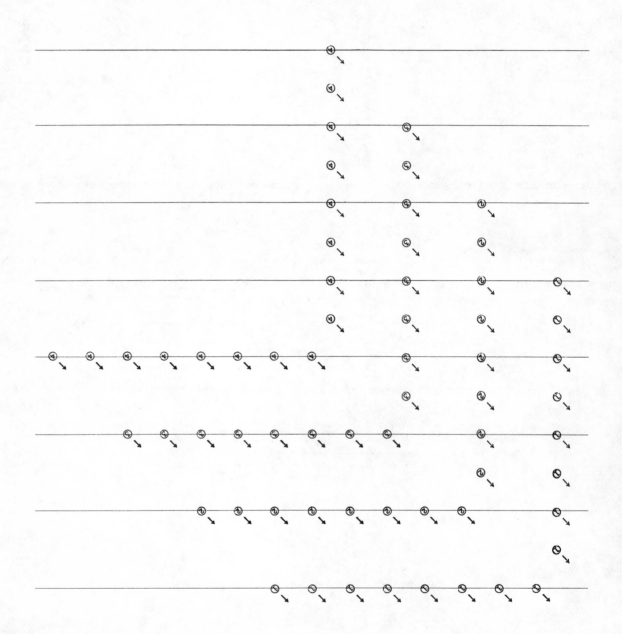

FIGURE 281—The movement continues.

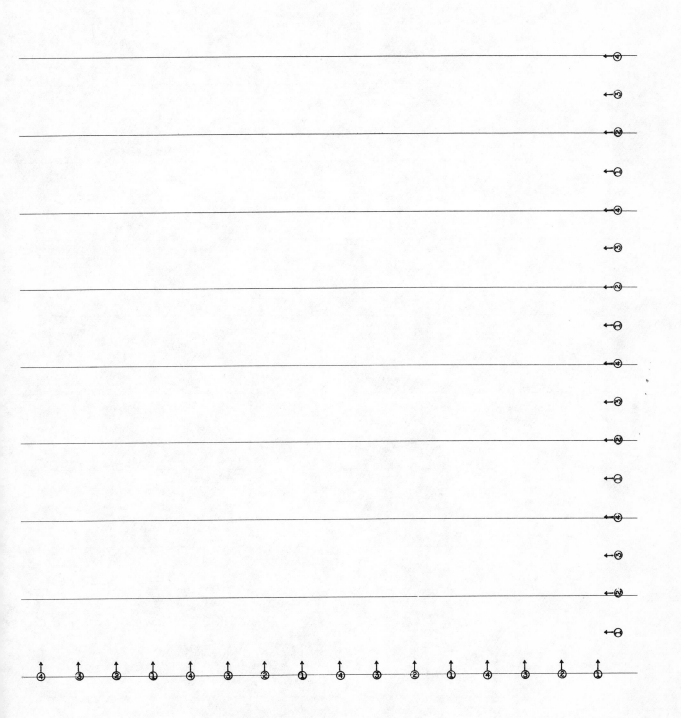

FIGURE 282—Both sides move forward.

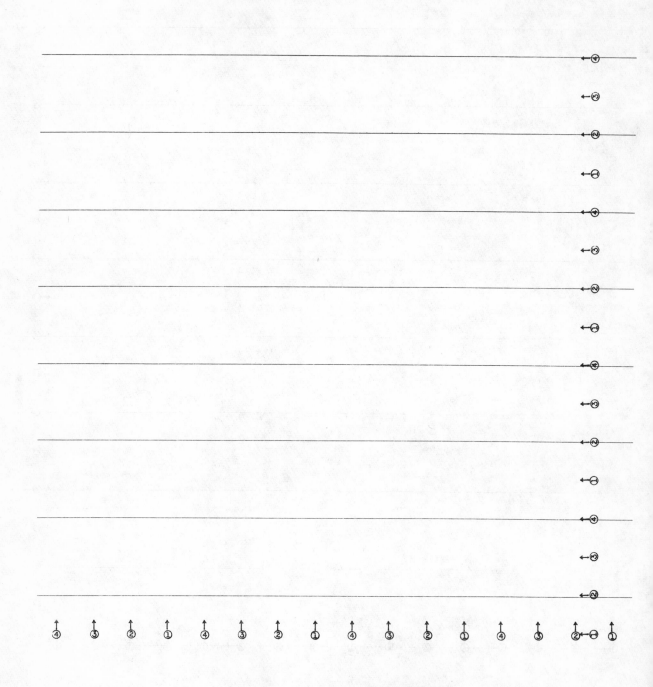

FIGURE 283—The movement continues.

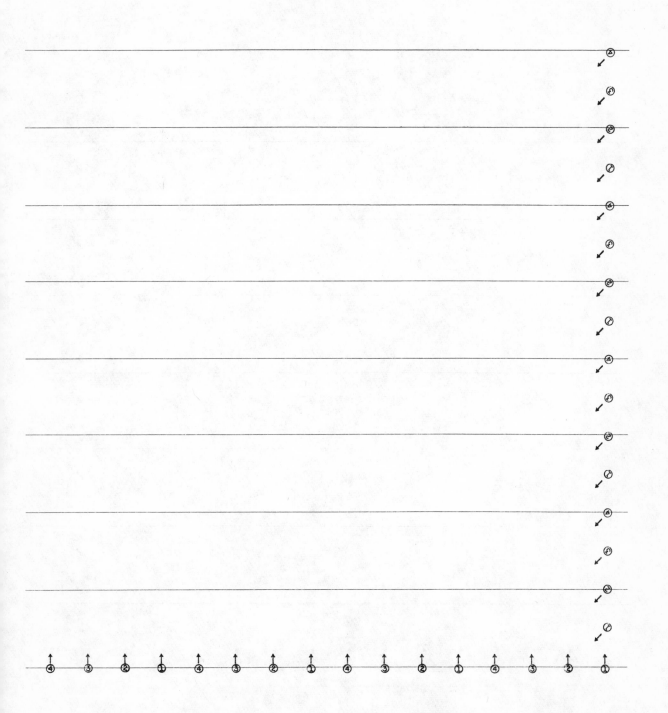

FIGURE 284—The sides move forward and at oblique.

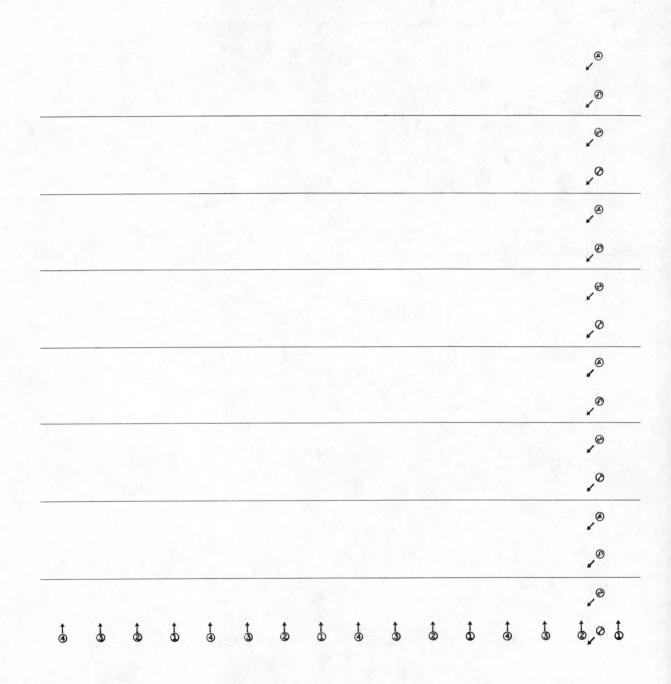

FIGURE 285—The movement continues.

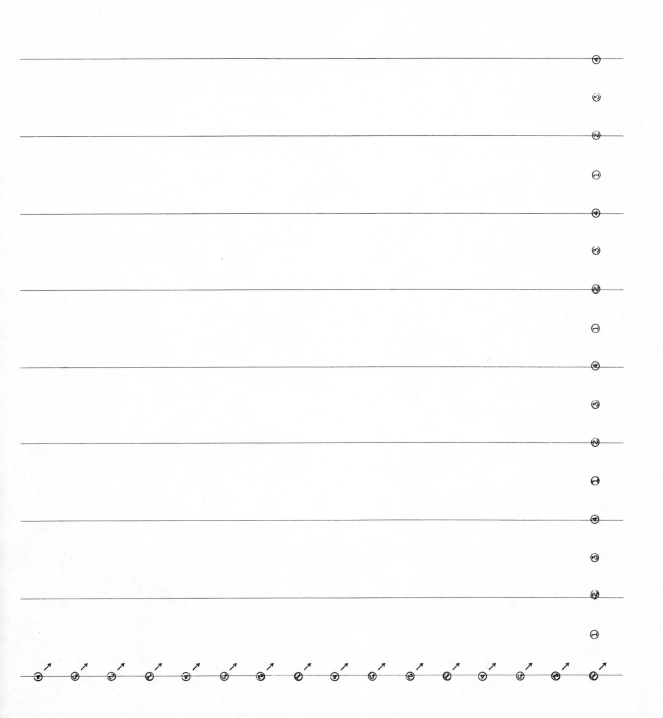

FIGURE 286—One side moves at oblique. The remaining side holds 2 steps and obliques.

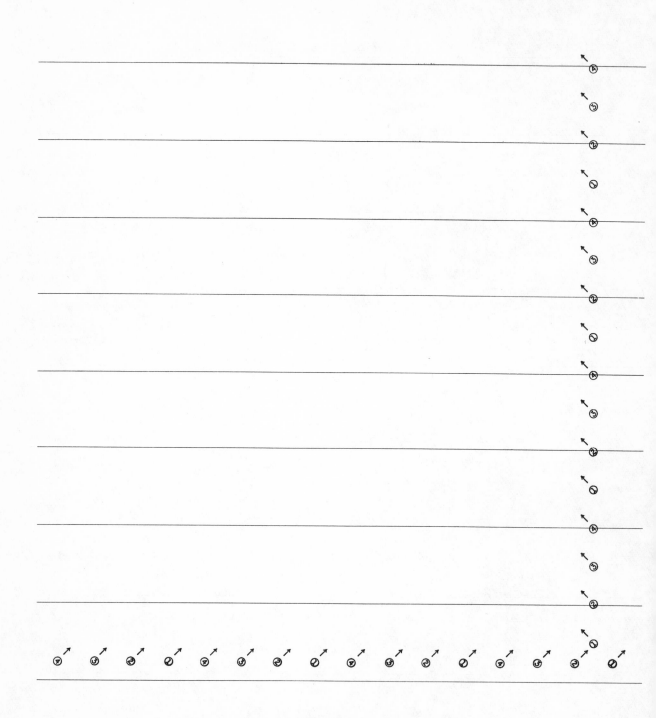

FIGURE 287—The movement continues.

FIGURE 288—A drill movement using multiple L's.

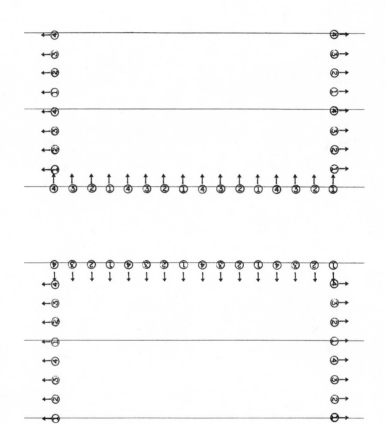

FIGURE 289—The movement continues.

The "T"

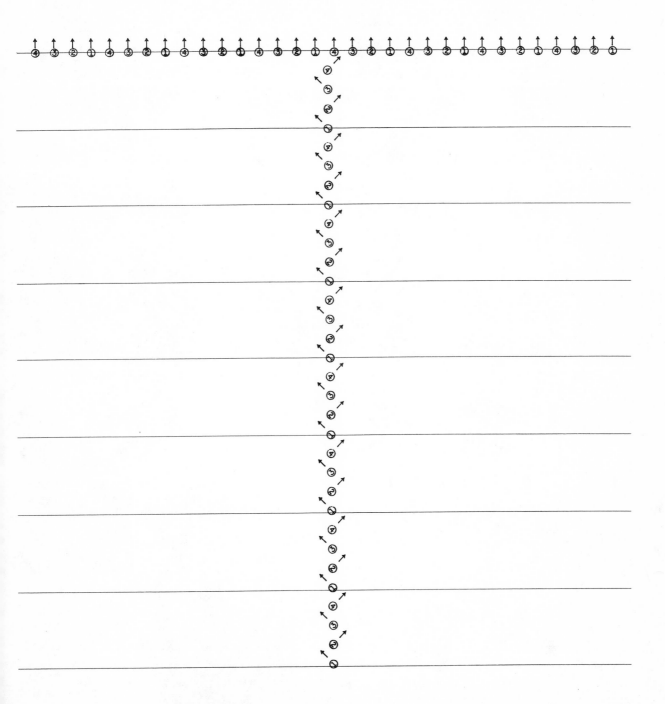

FIGURE 290—The top moves forward. The stem
divides and obliques to the outside.

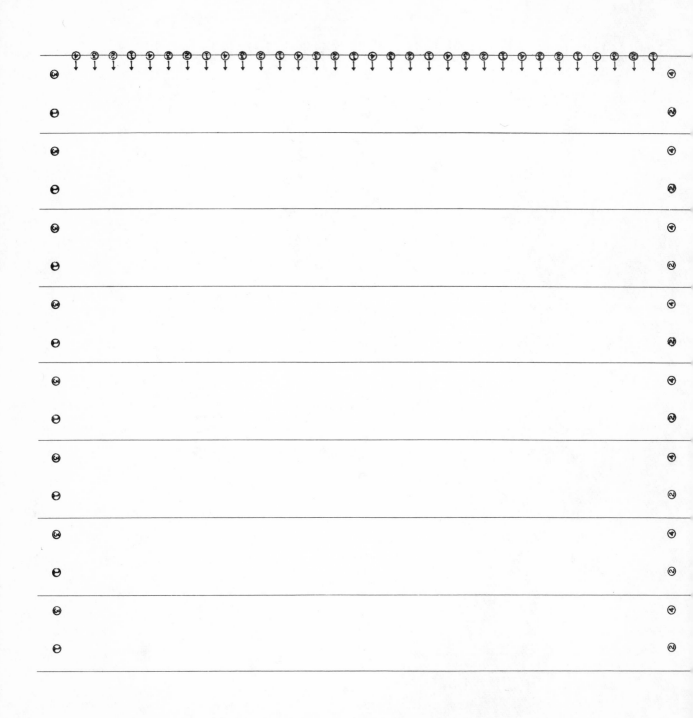

FIGURE 291—The top executes to-the-rear. The
obliquing lines face the center and hold.

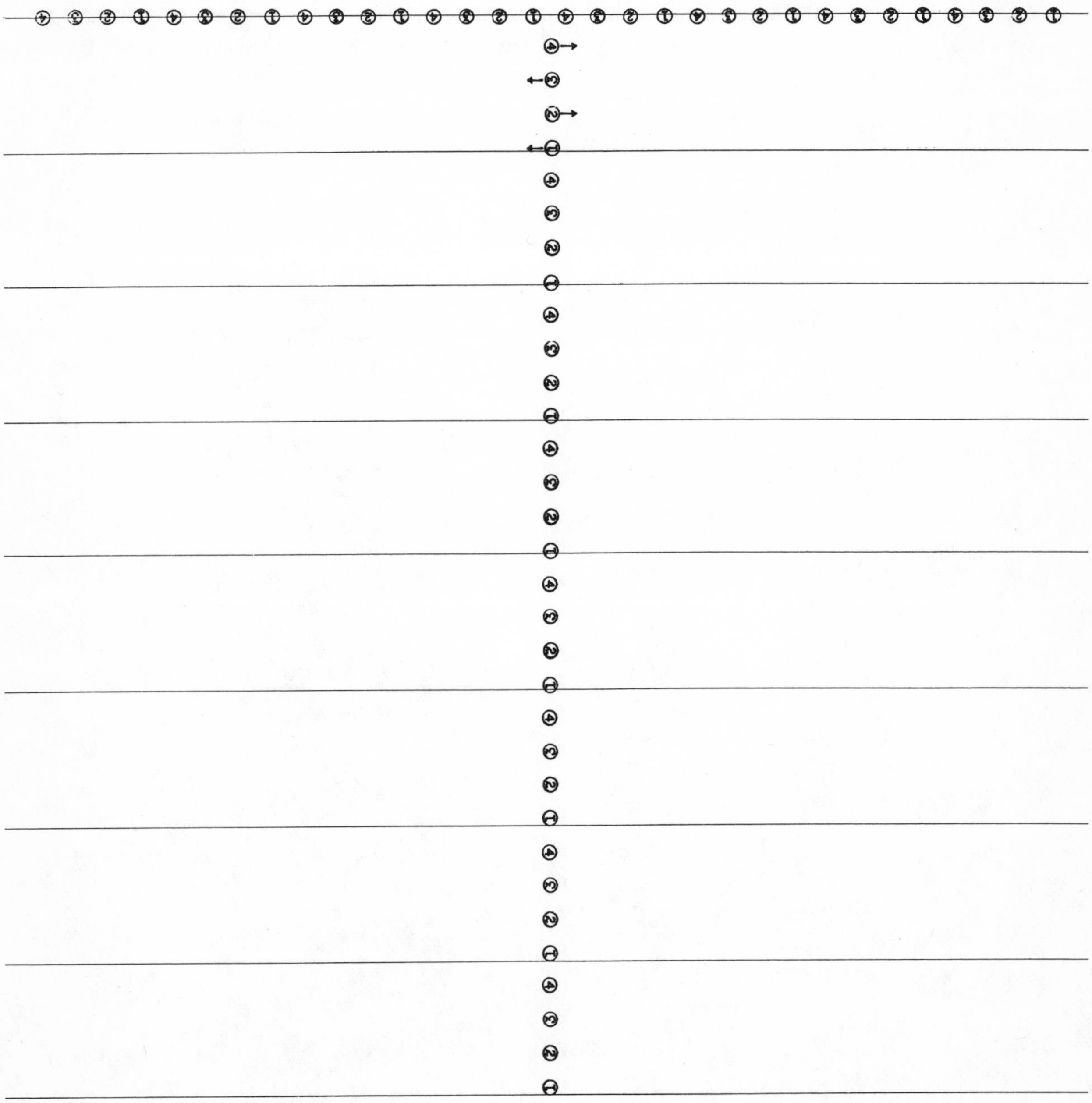

FIGURE 292—The stem executes step 8. The top
holds for 2 steps and executes step 2 from the
center.

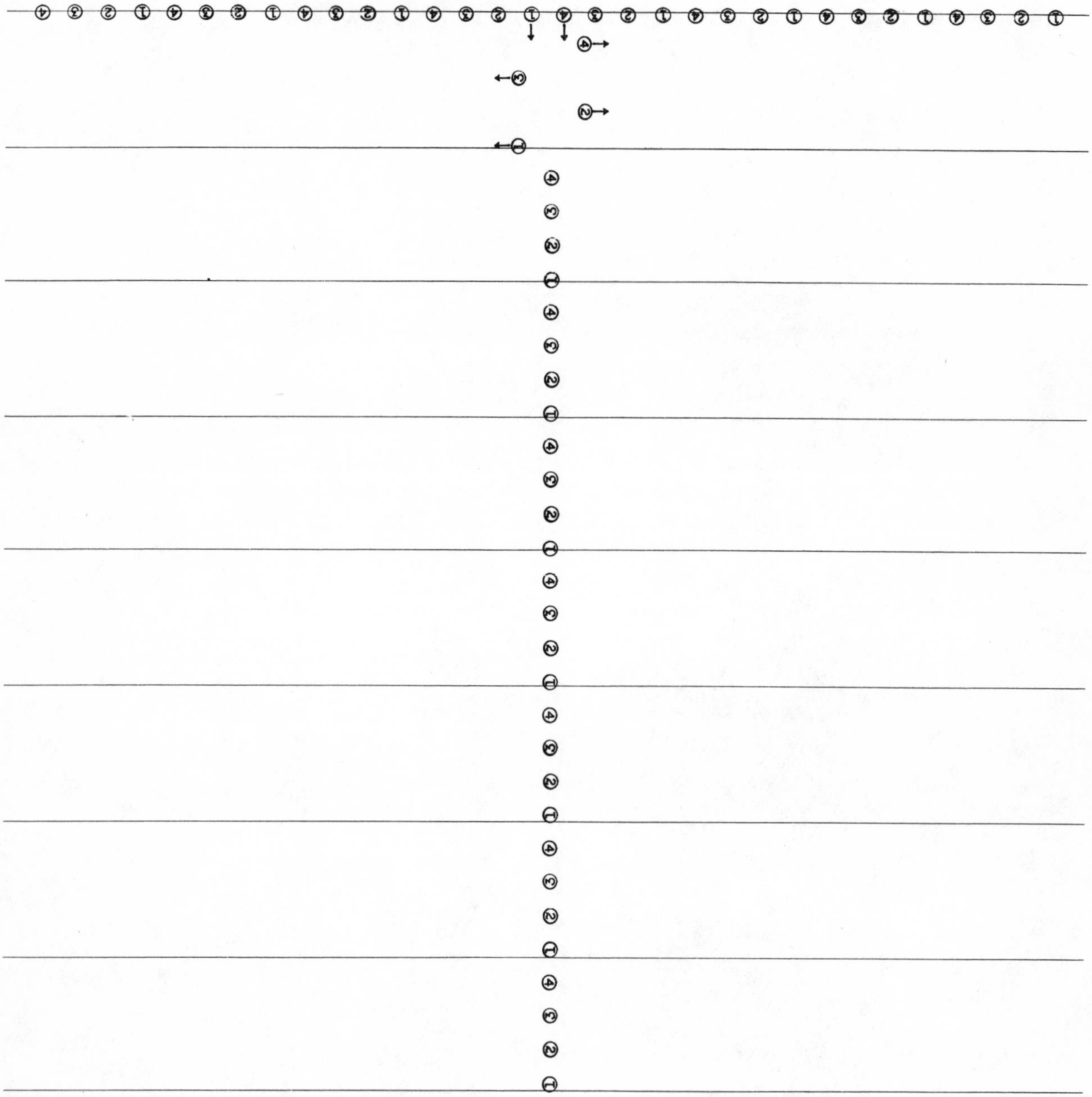

FIGURE 293—The movement continues.

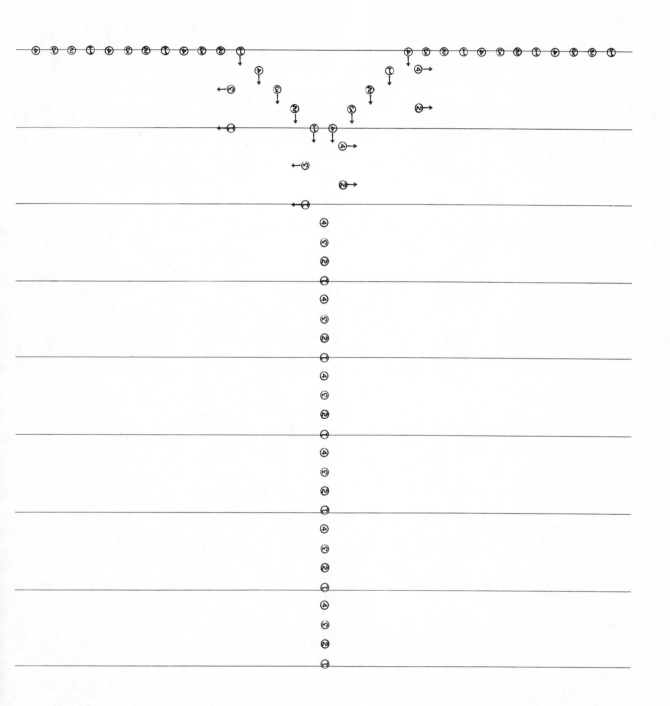

FIGURE 294—The movement continues.

FIGURE 295—The top moves forward. The stem moves in file.

FIGURE 296—The stem executes a flank 4 by squads.

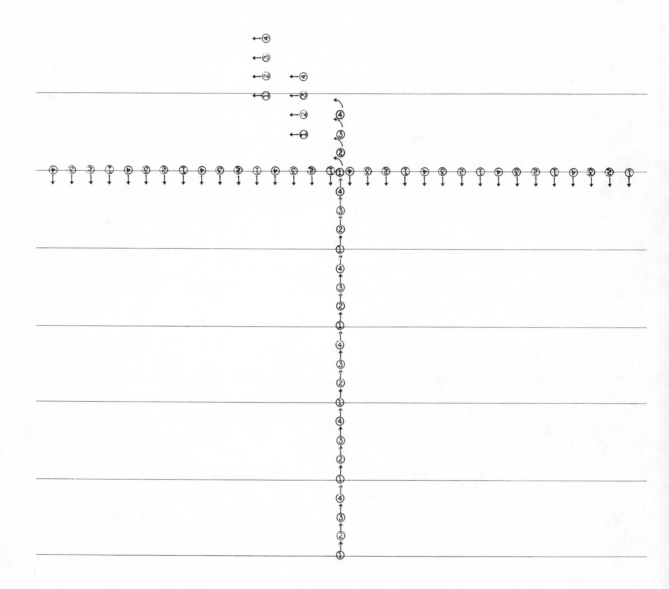

FIGURE 297—The movement continues.

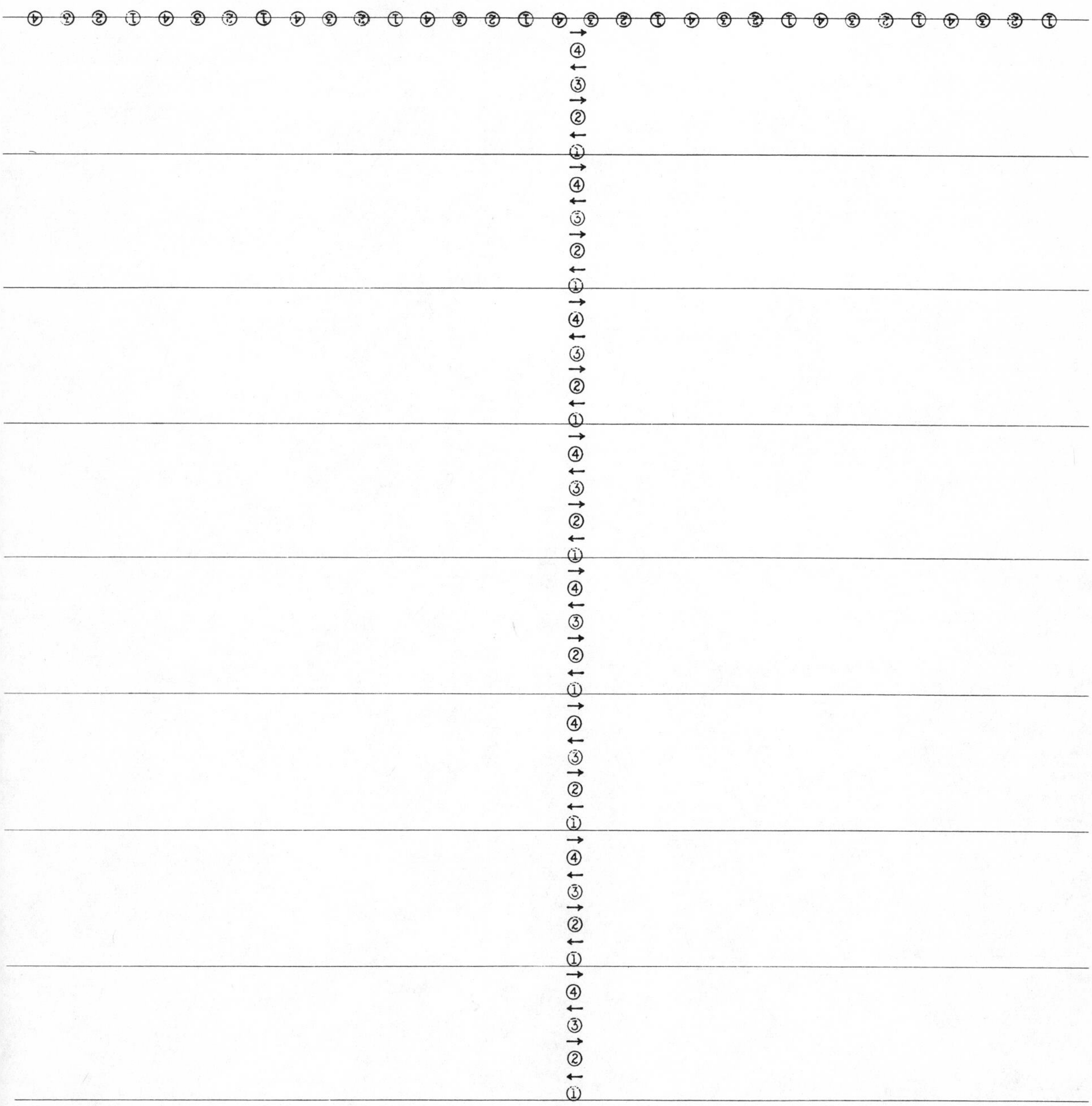

FIGURE 298—The stem executes side steps. The top holds for 2 steps and moves forward.

FIGURE 299—The top picks up the stem as it
moves forward.

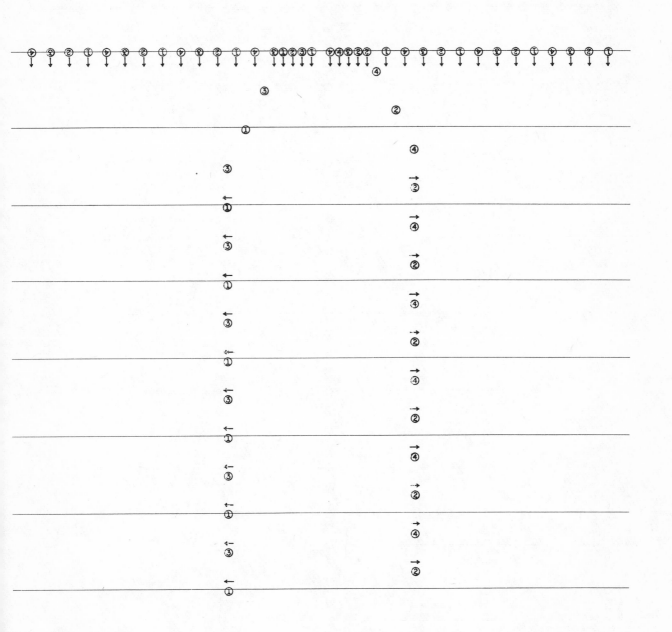

FIGURE 300—The movement continues.

FIGURE 301—The top holds. The stem turns 60
degrees and obliques through the top.

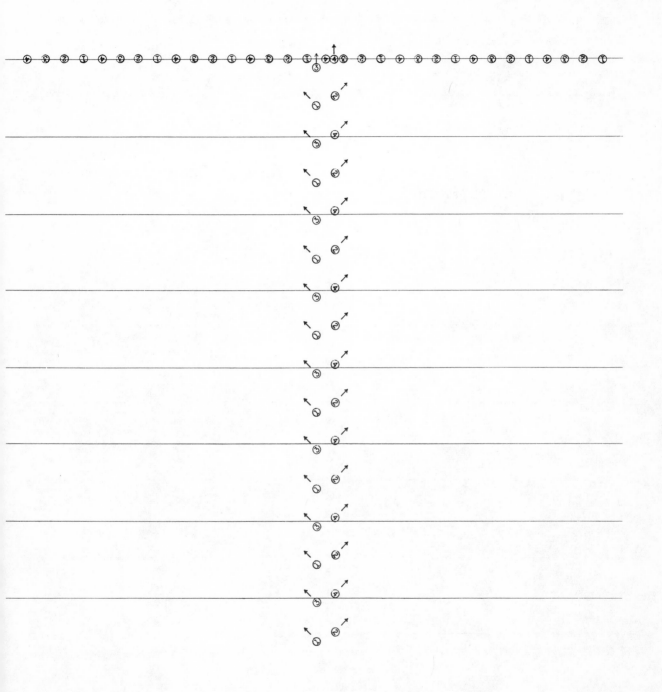

FIGURE 302—The movement continues.

FIGURE 303—The top holds for 2 steps and moves
forward. The stem turns 45 degrees and obliques
through the top.

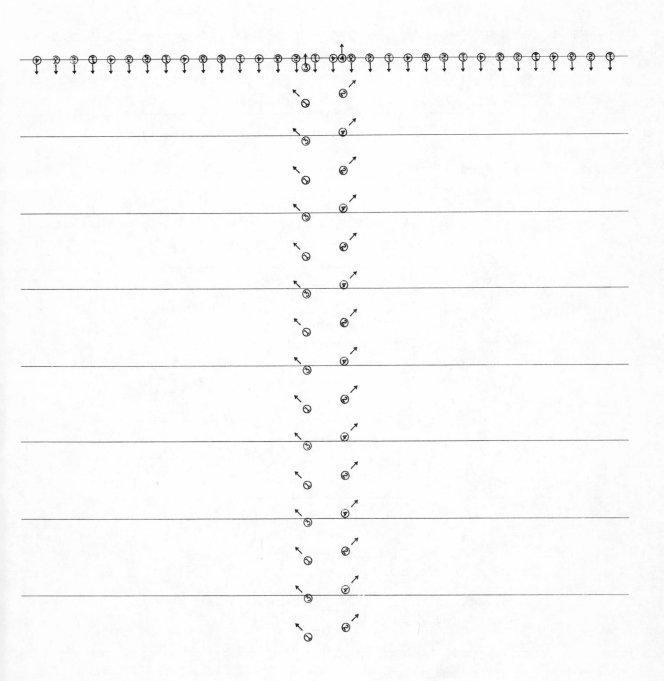

FIGURE 304—The movement continues.

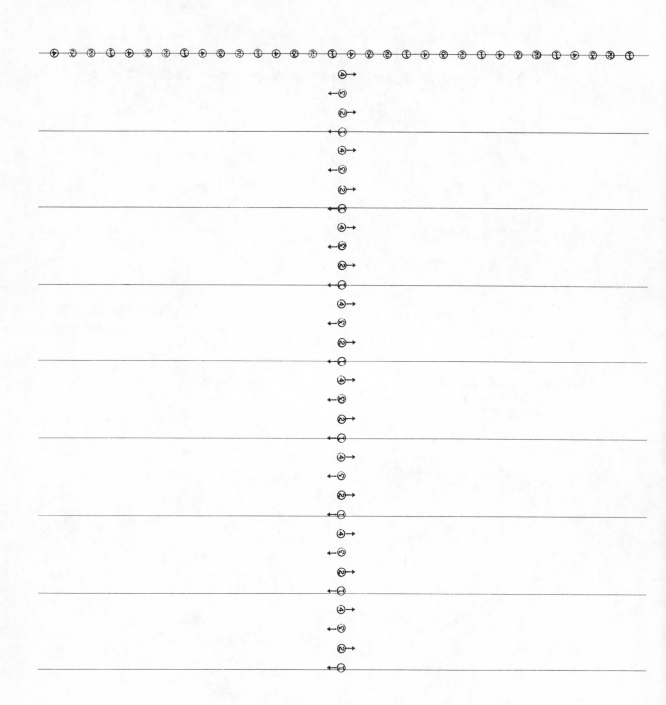

FIGURE 305—The top holds for 2 steps and moves forward. The stem moves forward for 2 steps and executes flank 2 continuing the forward motion at half step.

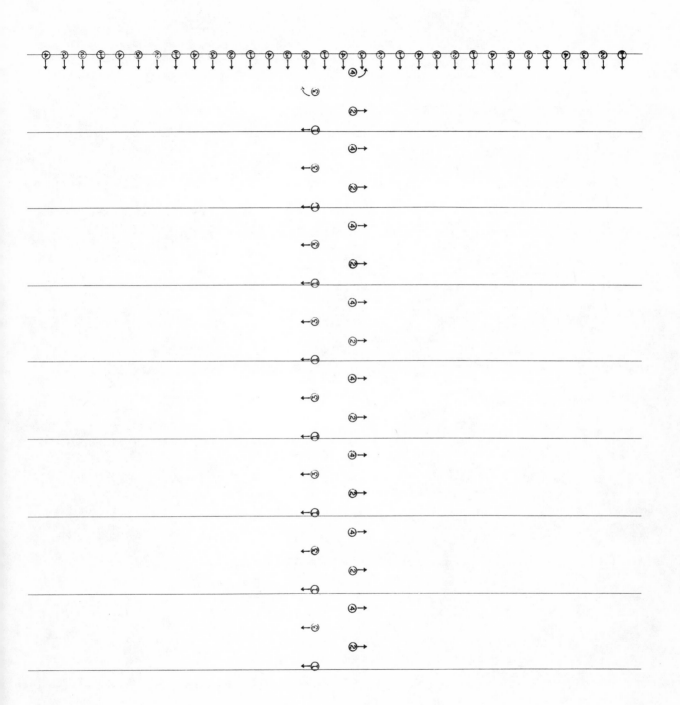

FIGURE 306—The movement continues.

FIGURE 307—The top holds for a definite number of steps. The stem obliques for a definite number of steps and executes a 135 degree turn and moves through the top.

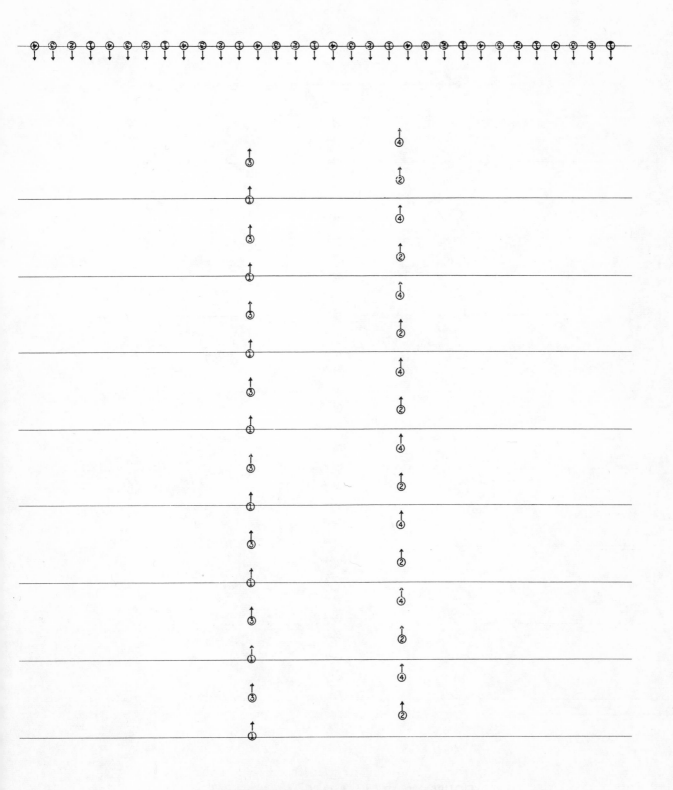

FIGURE 308—The movement continues.

FIGURE 309—The top holds for a definite number
of steps. The stem moves forward.

FIGURE 310—The top moves forward as the stem
clears the way.

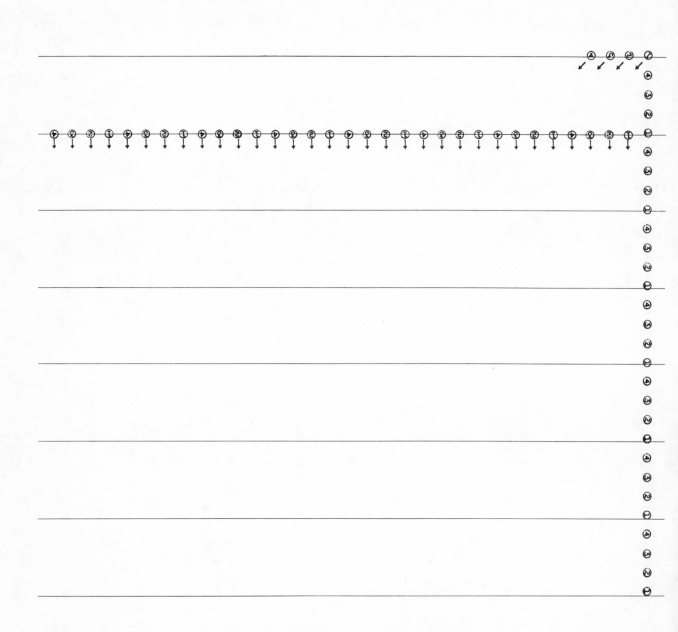

FIGURE 311—The stem executes step 2 with a 225
degree turn and obliques on to line.

FIGURE 312—The top executes step 2. The stem moves forward in file.

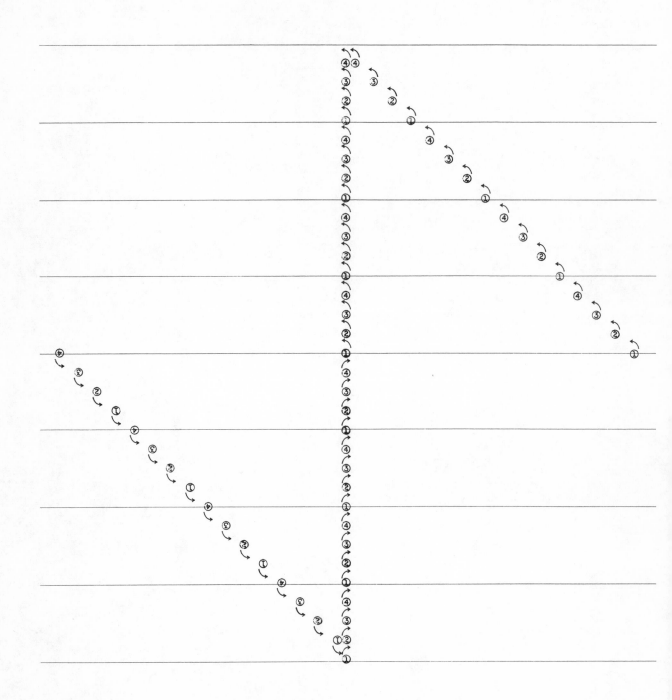

FIGURE 313—The top sections turn and move on
line. The stem turns and holds.

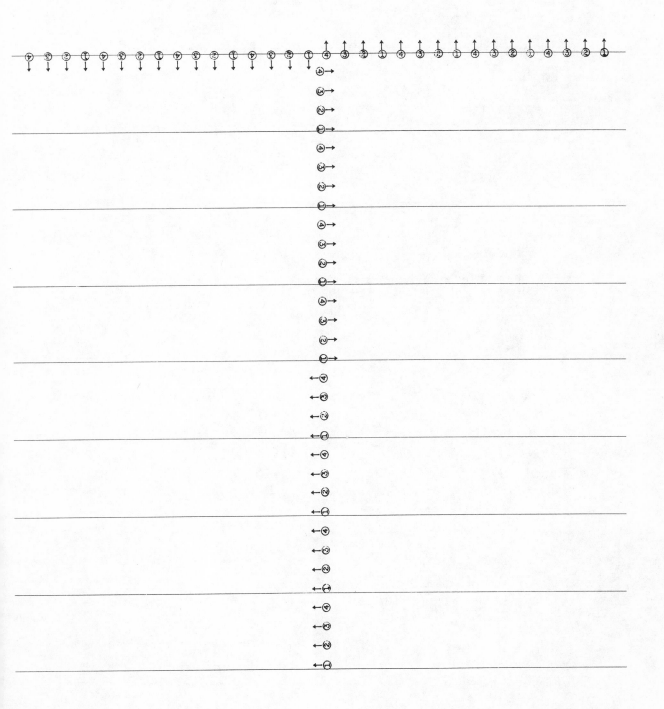

FIGURE 314—The top splits into 2 sections and
moves forward. The stem splits into 2 sections and
moves forward.

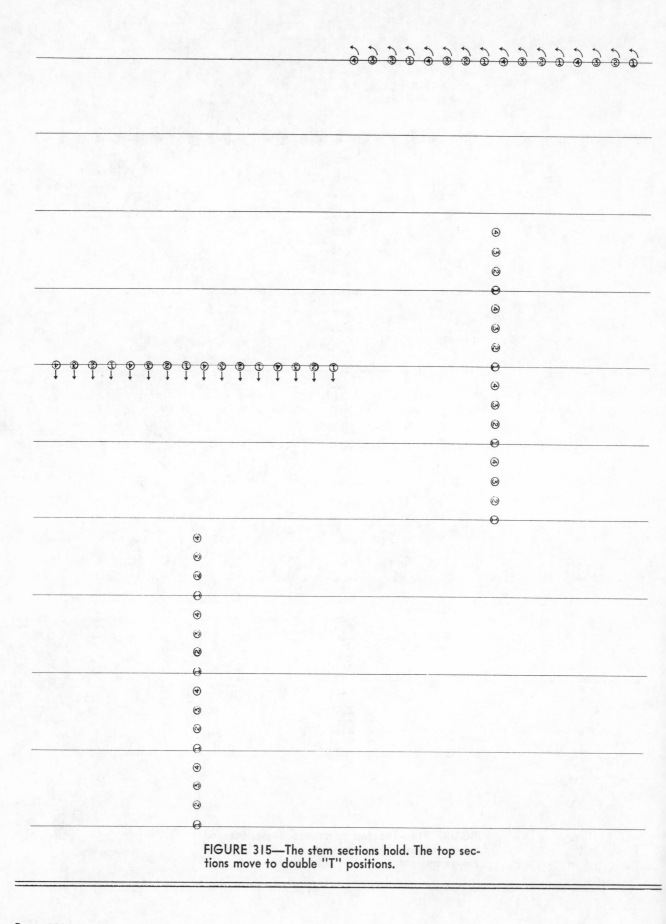

FIGURE 315—The stem sections hold. The top sections move to double "T" positions.

FIGURE 316—The top executes step 2 from the
center. The stem holds for a definite number of
steps and executes step 4 by twos.

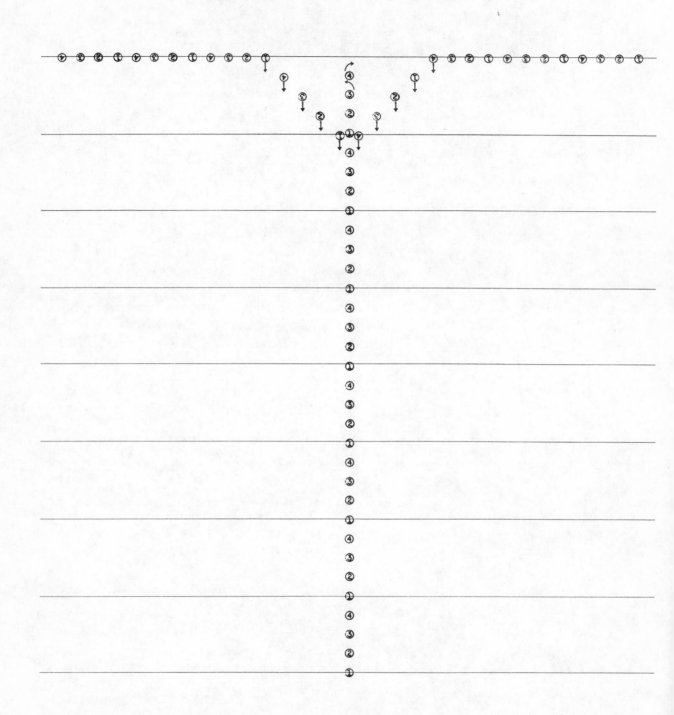

FIGURE 317—The movement continues.

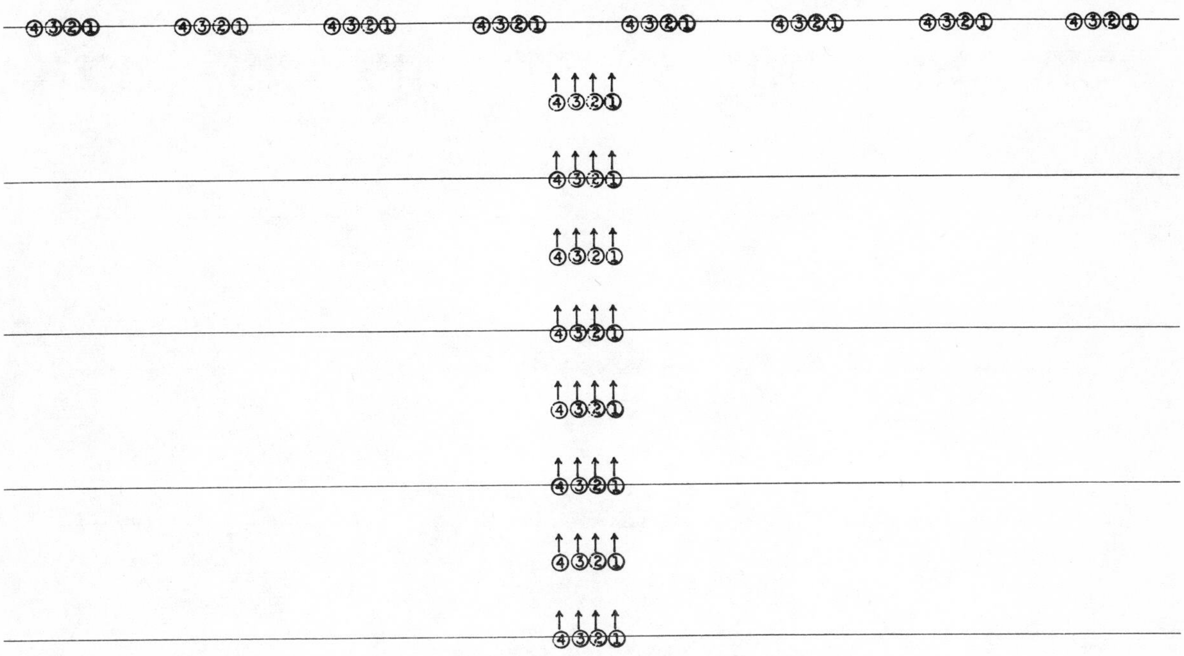

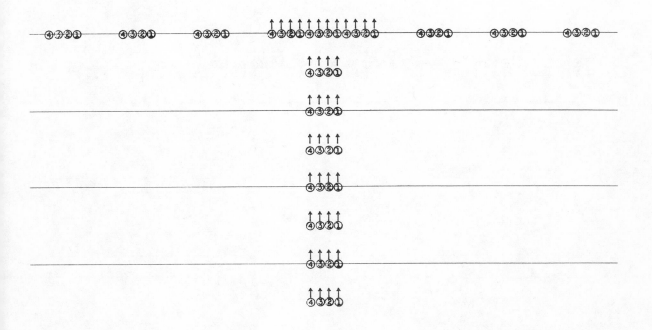

FIGURE 318—The top holds for a definite number of steps and executes step 4 from the center by squads. The stem moves forward.

FIGURE 319—The movement continues.

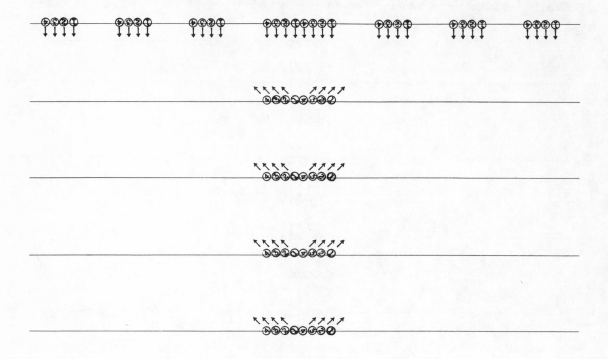

FIGURE 320—The top moves forward. The stem
obliques to the left and to the right by squads.

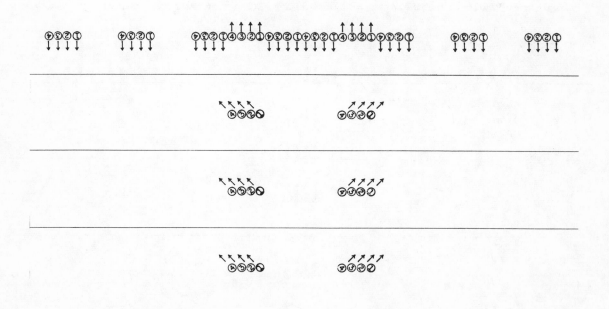

FIGURE 321—The movement continues.

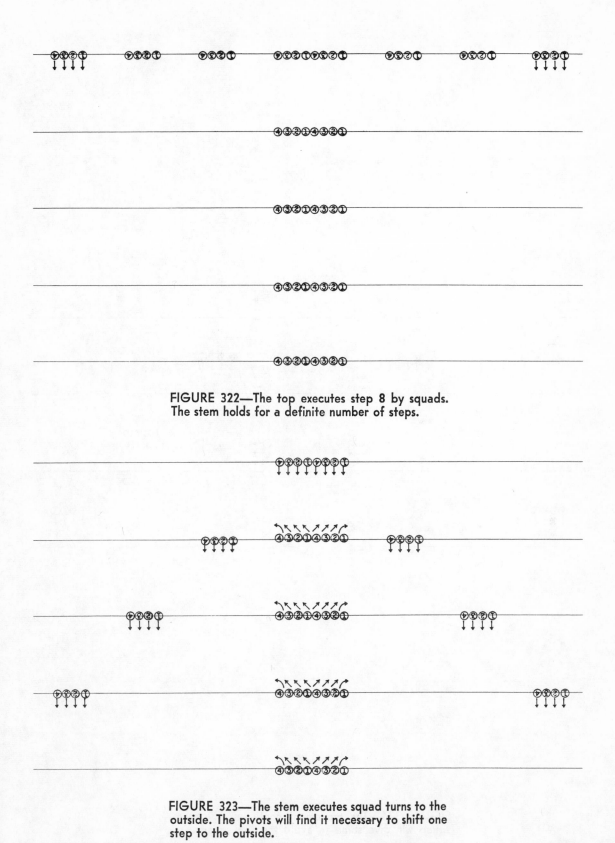

FIGURE 322—The top executes step 8 by squads.
The stem holds for a definite number of steps.

FIGURE 323—The stem executes squad turns to the
outside. The pivots will find it necessary to shift one
step to the outside.

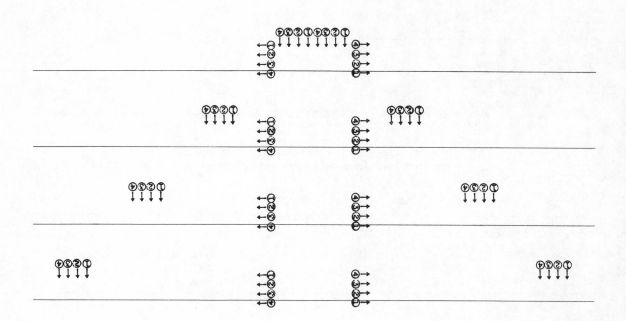

FIGURE 324—The movement continues. The stem
squad will give some to avoid the top squads.

The Cross

FIGURE 325—One line holds. The other line obliques on center pivot.

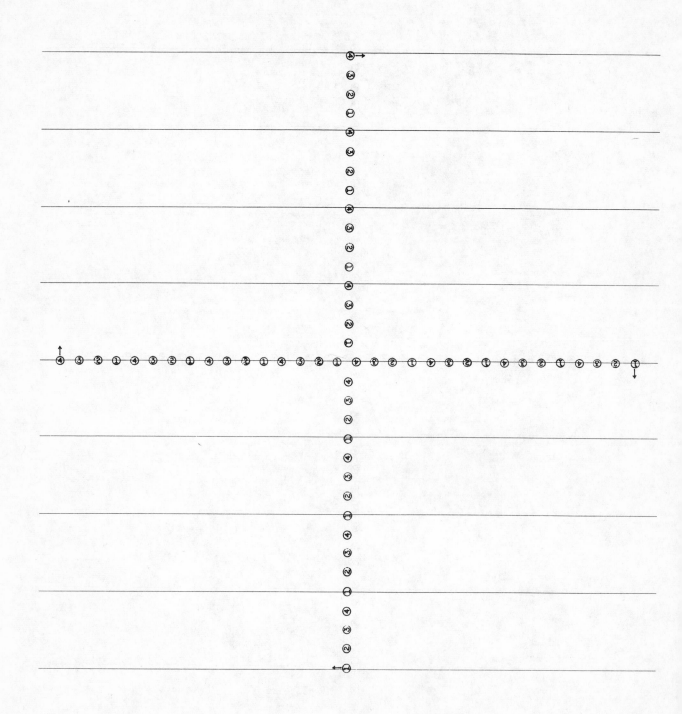

FIGURE 326—Each spoke executes step 2.

FIGURE 327—Each spoke flanks and moves on a
new line.

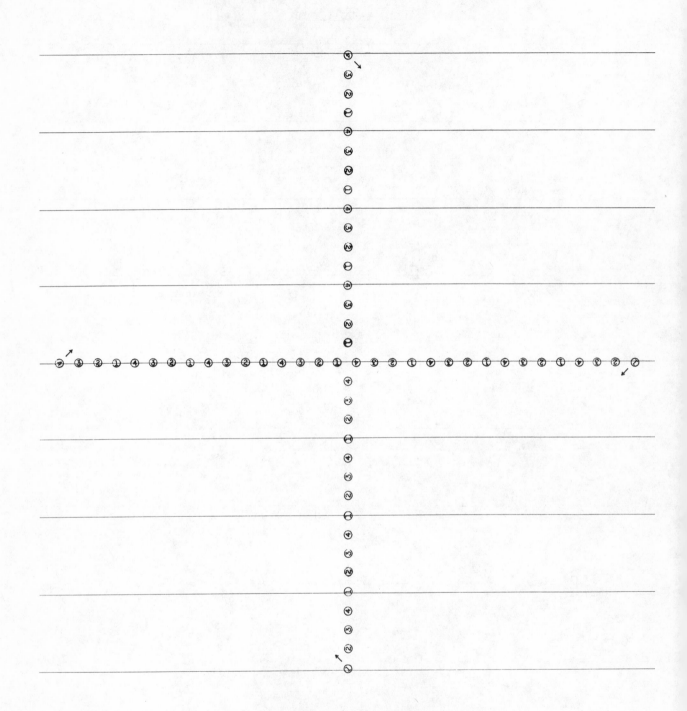

FIGURE 328—Each spoke executes step 2 and
moves on to a new line at oblique.

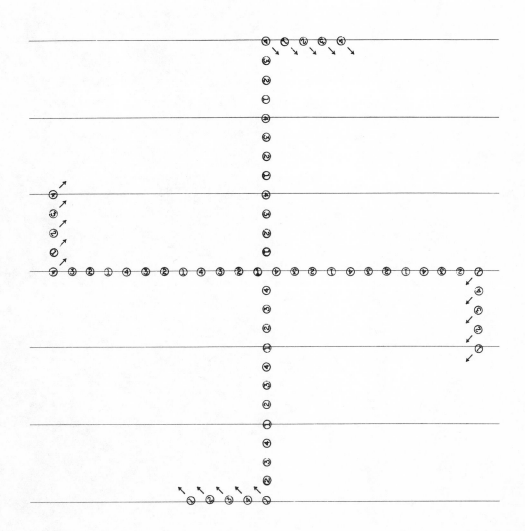

FIGURE 329—The movement continues.

FIGURE 330—Each spoke obliques on to a new line.

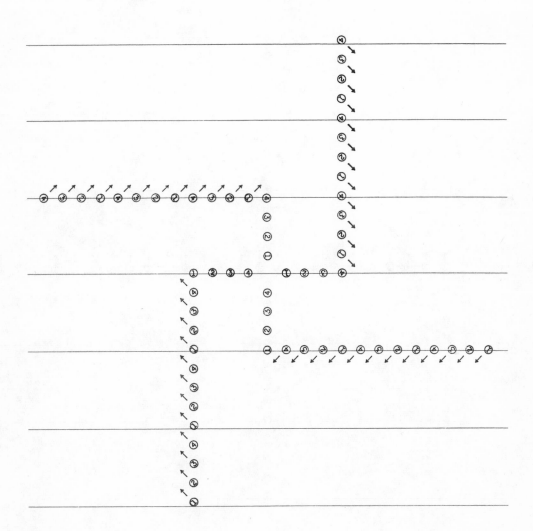

FIGURE 331—The movement continues.

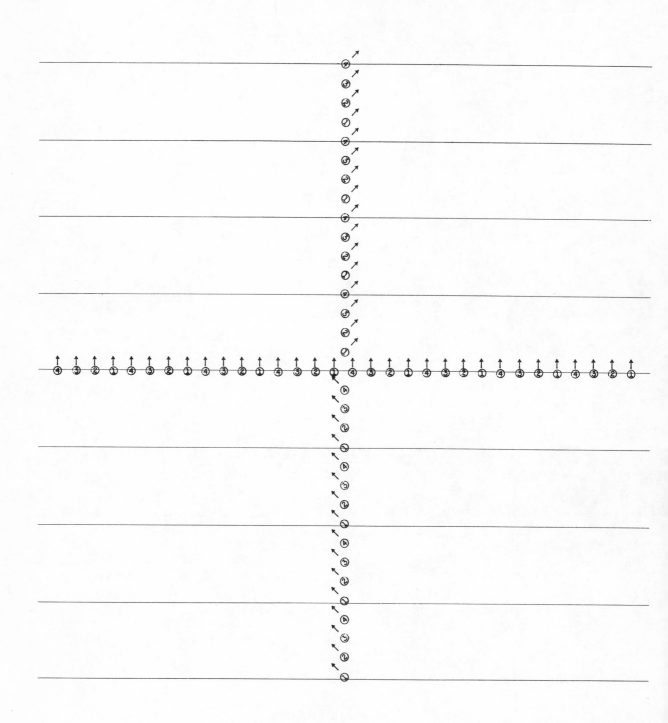

FIGURE 332—The crossbar moves forward. The other spokes oblique for a definite number of steps and change oblique in a series.

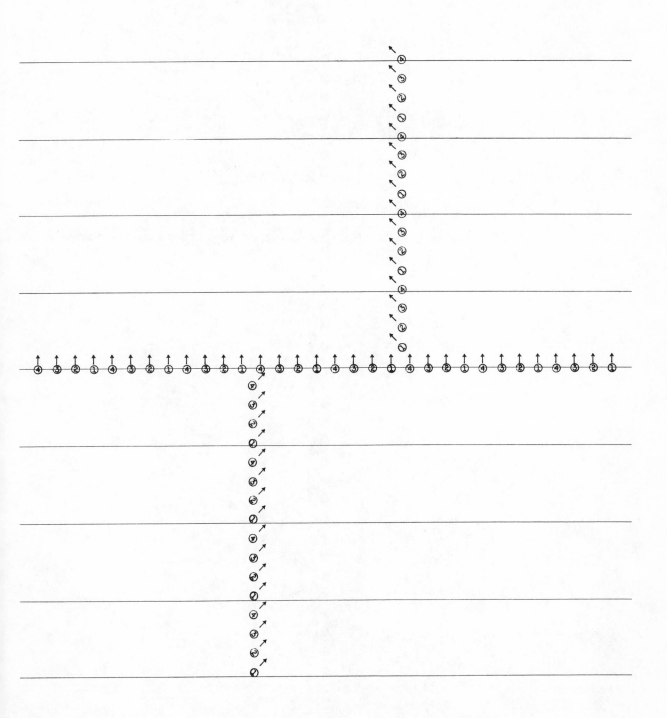

FIGURE 333—The movement continues.

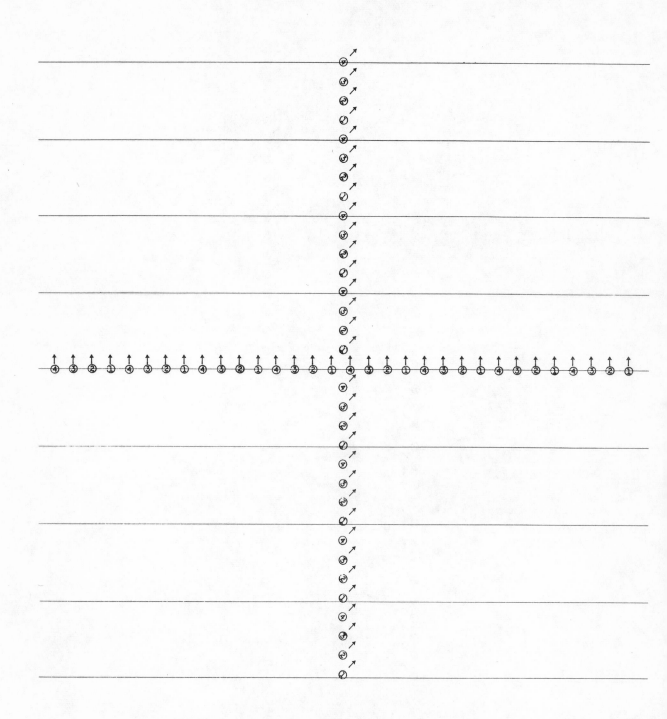

FIGURE 334—The movement continues.

FIGURE 335—The movement continues.

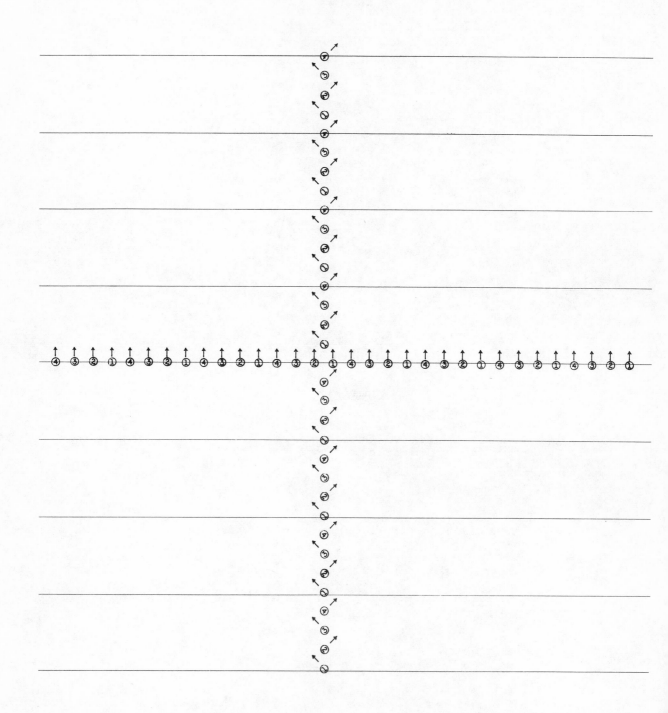

FIGURE 336—The movement continues.

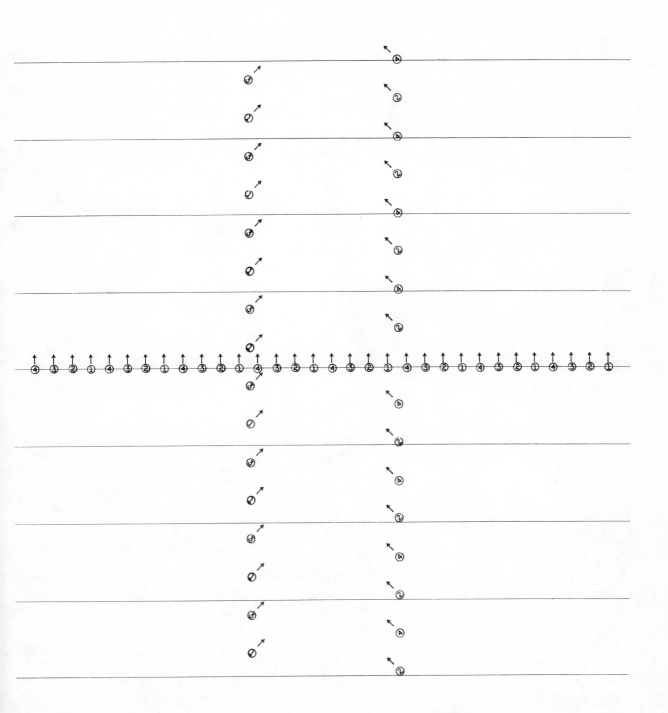

FIGURE 337—The movement continues.

FIGURE 338—Each spoke executes step 2 and moves on to a new line.

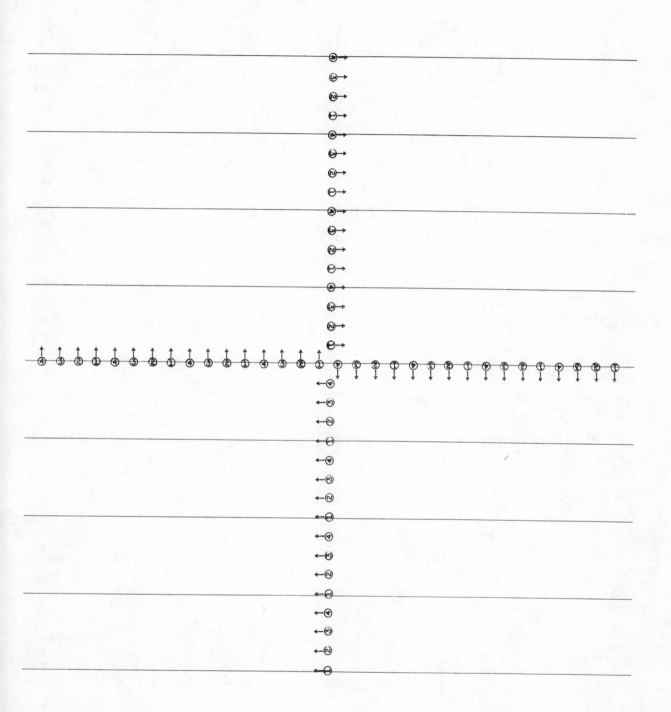

FIGURE 339—Each spoke moves forward 32 steps
and executes a 135 degree turn.

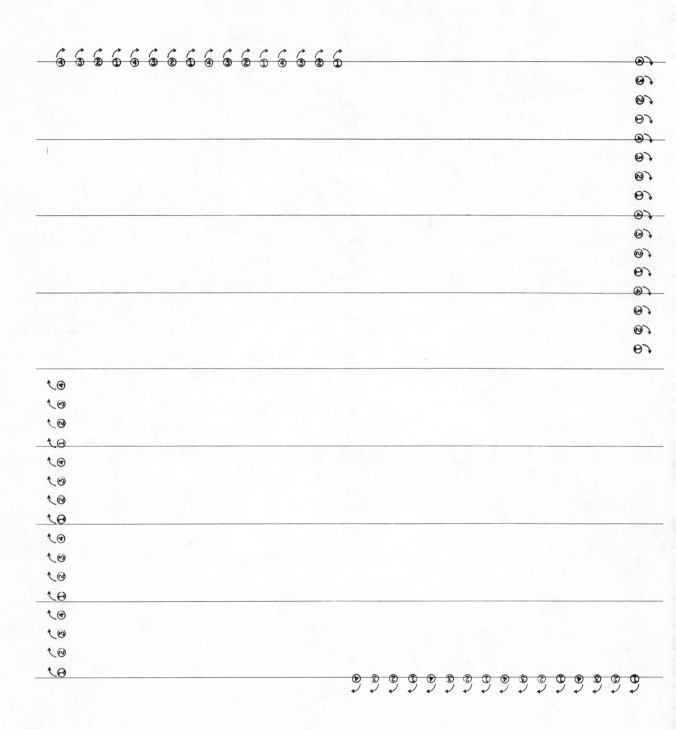

FIGURE 340—The spokes are in position to execute the turn.

FIGURE 341—The spokes oblique on to a new line.

FIGURE 342—Spokes move out at oblique as corners.

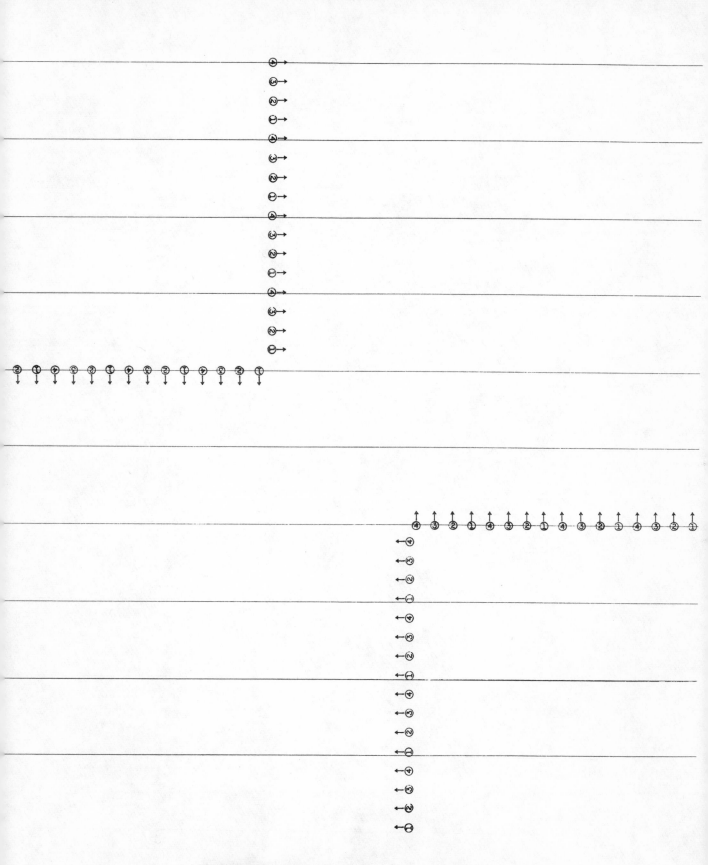

FIGURE 343—Each spoke turns and moves forward
to join adjacent spoke.

FIGURE 344—Spokes join to form corner and oblique back to original position.

FIGURE 345—Each spoke executes step 2.

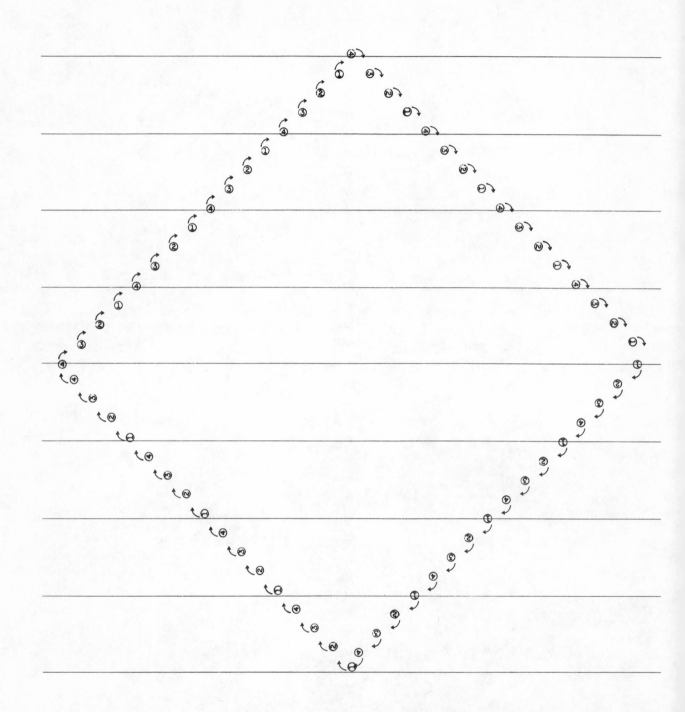

FIGURE 346—The unit is in a square formation and can execute movements as a square or can turn toward a diagonal and form a meshed line.

FIGURE 347—Each spoke obliques and meshes with
adjacent spoke.

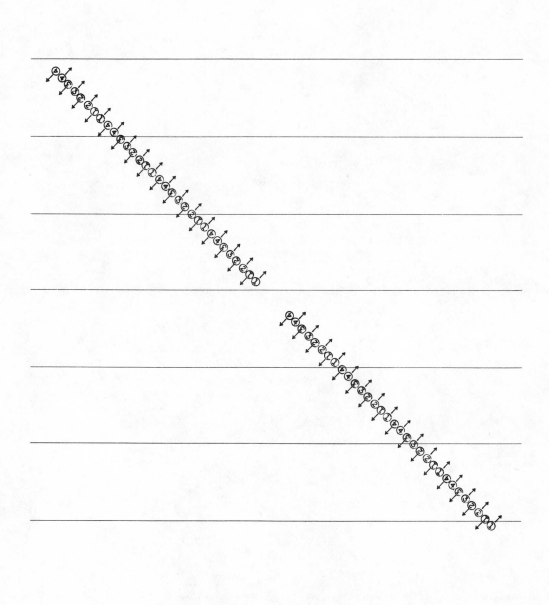

FIGURE 348—The movement continues.

FIGURE 349—The spokes oblique away from the
center.

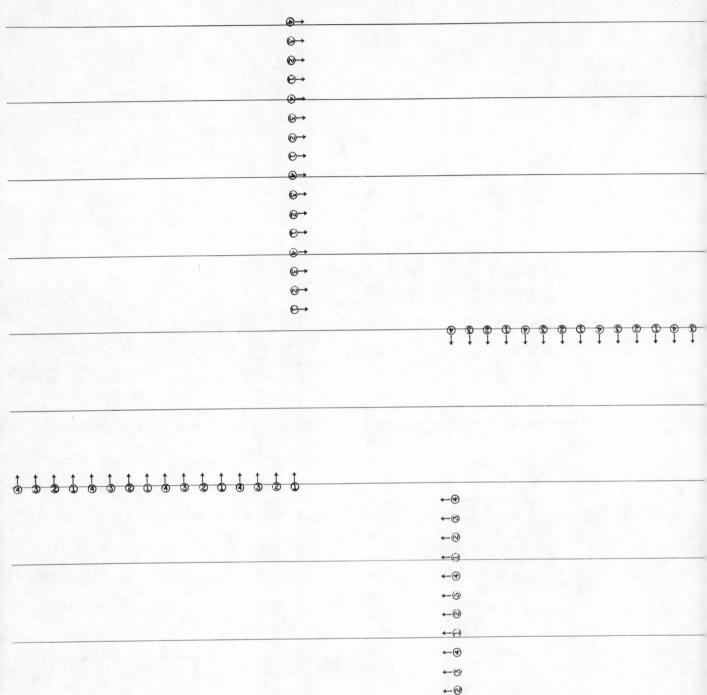

FIGURE 350—The spokes execute a 135 degree
turn and move forward a definite number of steps.

FIGURE 351—The spokes execute a 135 degree
turn and move back to original position.

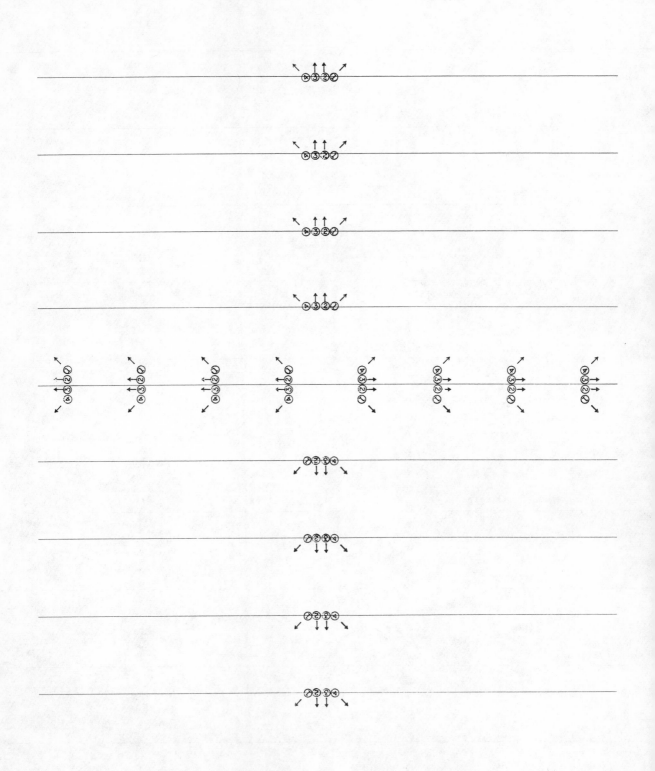

FIGURE 352—Each squad executes flank 2 from both sides.

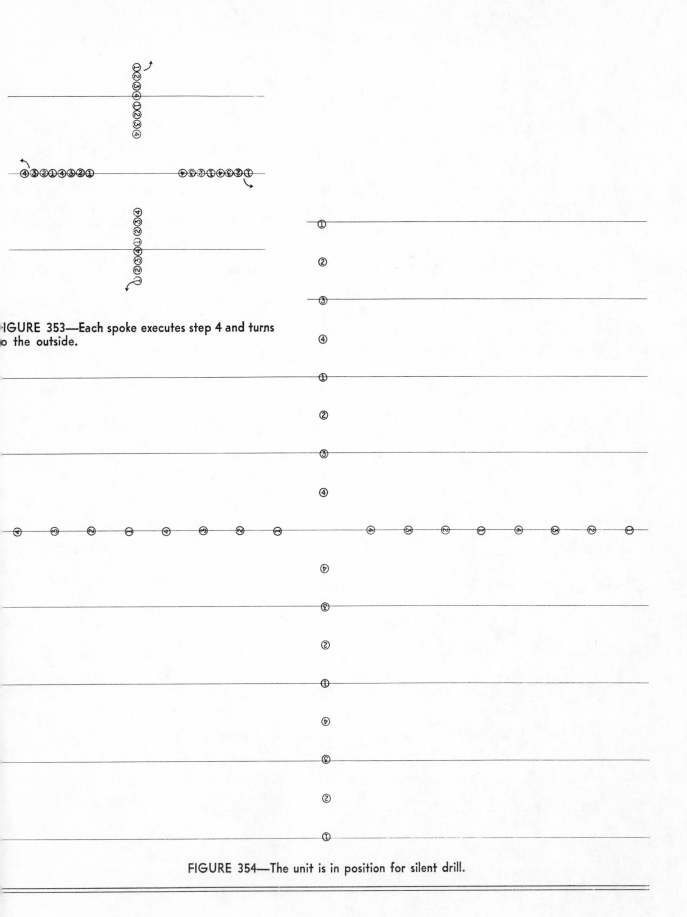

FIGURE 353—Each spoke executes step 4 and turns to the outside.

FIGURE 354—The unit is in position for silent drill.

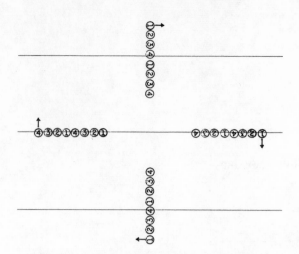

FIGURE 355—Each spoke executes step 4.

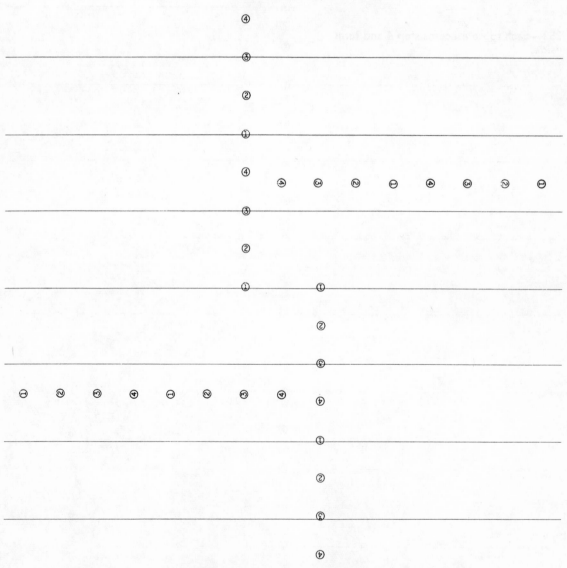

FIGURE 356—The unit is in position for silent drill.

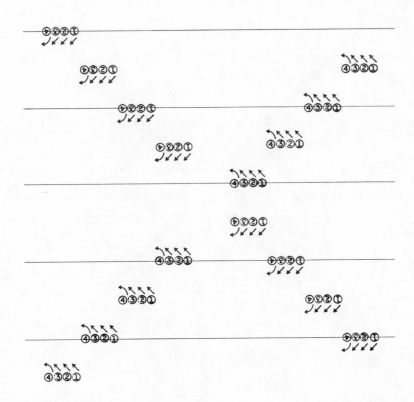

FIGURE 357—Each squad executes a half squad turn.

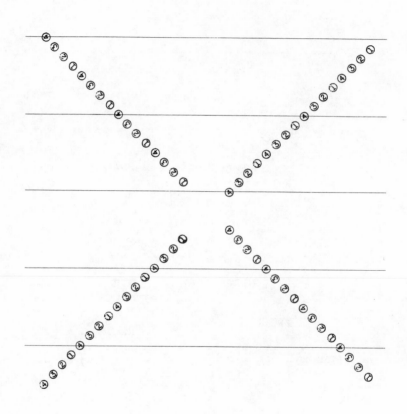

FIGURE 358—The movement is complete.

The Diamond

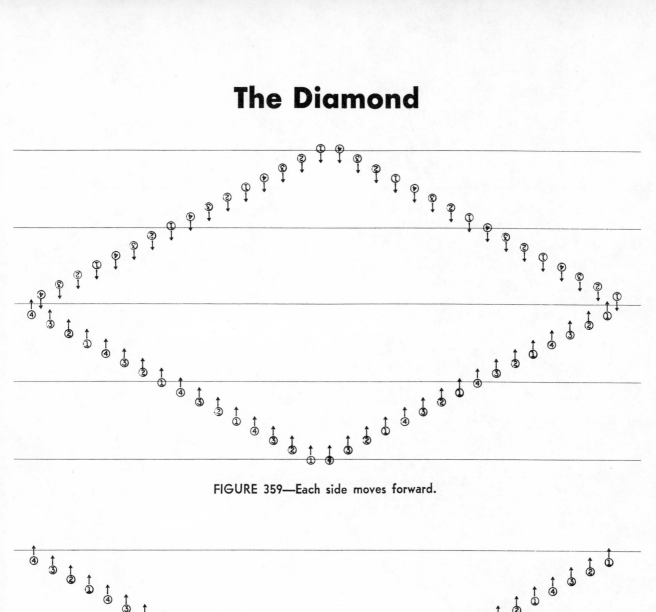

FIGURE 359—Each side moves forward.

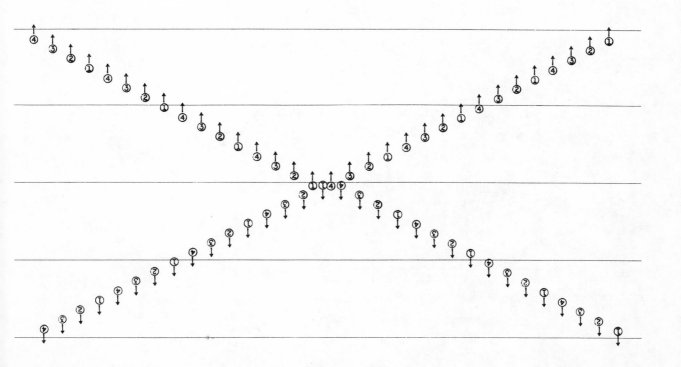

FIGURE 360—The movement continues.

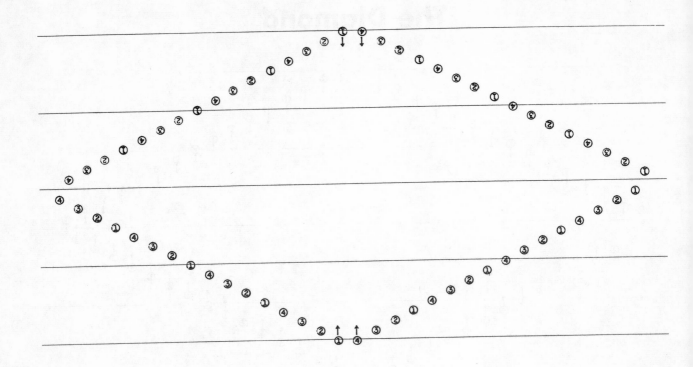

FIGURE 361—Each side executes step 2 from the center.

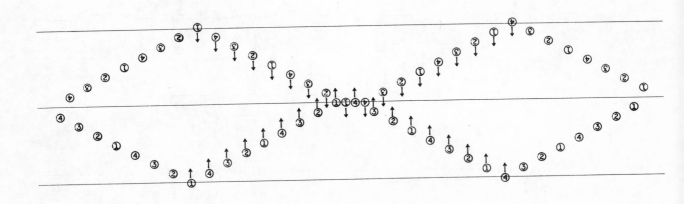

FIGURE 362—The movement continues.

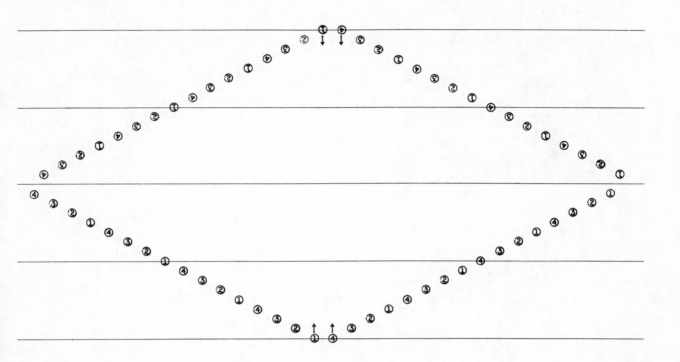

FIGURE 363—Each side executes a peel from the center.

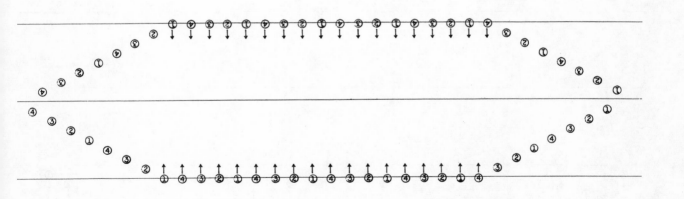

FIGURE 364—The movement continues.

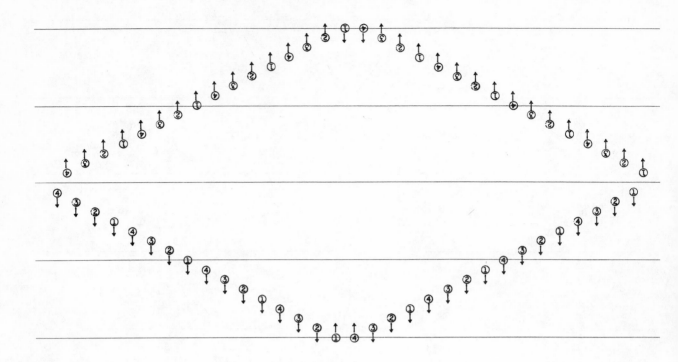

FIGURE 365—Each side moves backward and executes step 2 from the center.

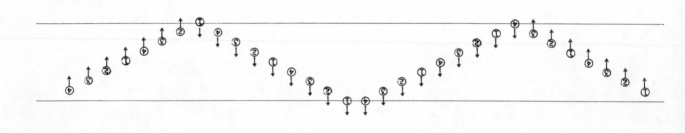

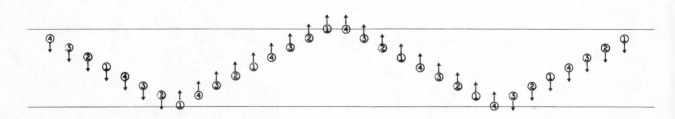

FIGURE 366—The movement continues.

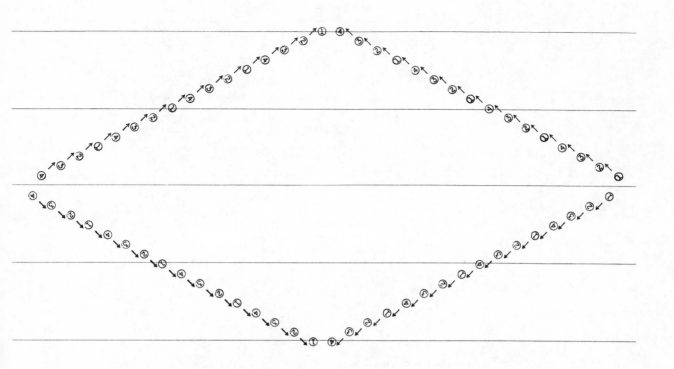

FIGURE 367—Each side obliques on to line.

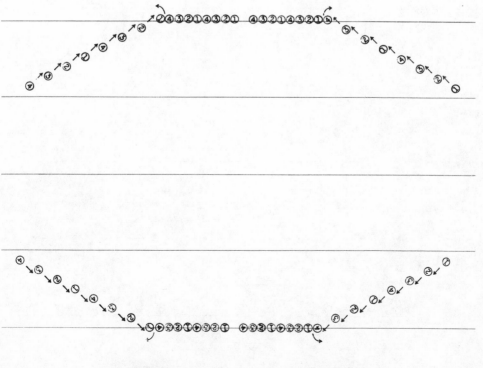

FIGURE 368—The movement continues.

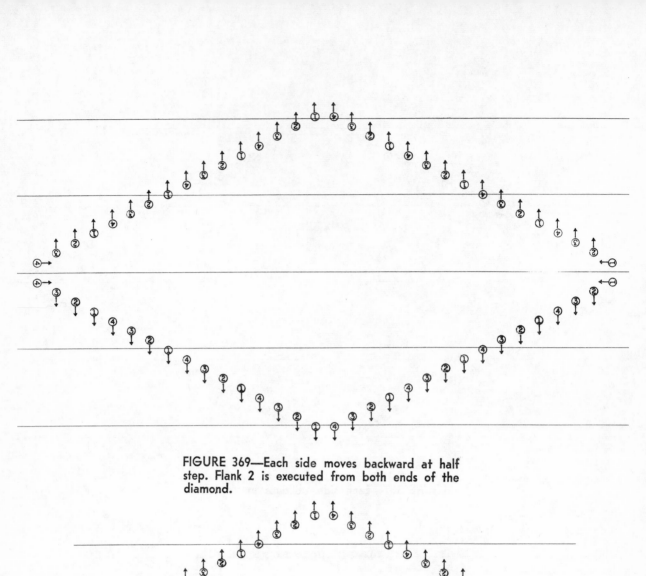

FIGURE 369—Each side moves backward at half step. Flank 2 is executed from both ends of the diamond.

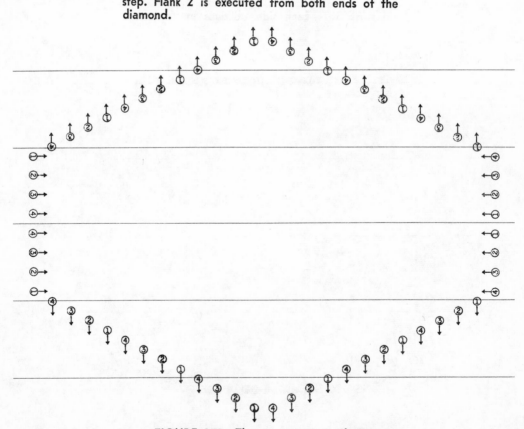

FIGURE 370—The movement continues.

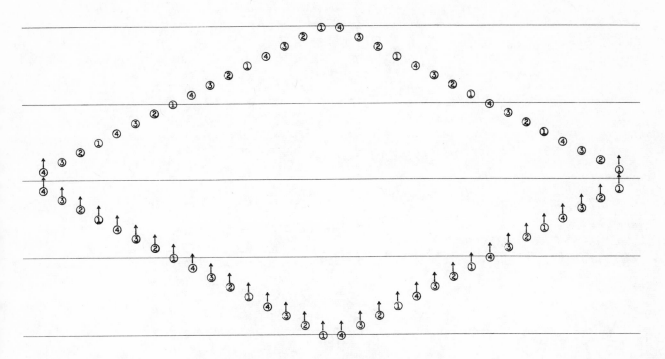

FIGURE 371—One side moves forward. The remaining side executes step 2 from both ends.

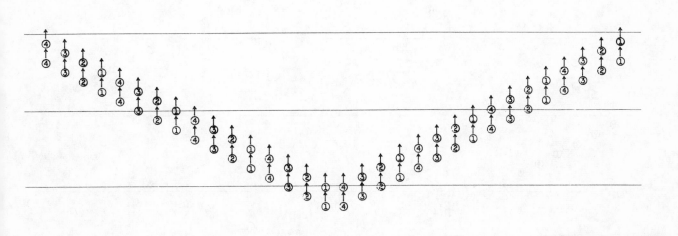

FIGURE 372—The movement continues.

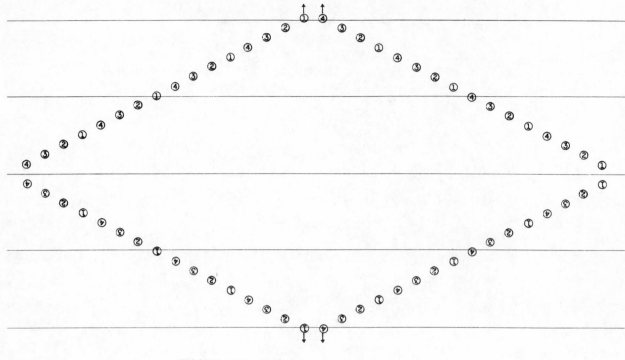

FIGURE 373—Each side executes a peel from the center.

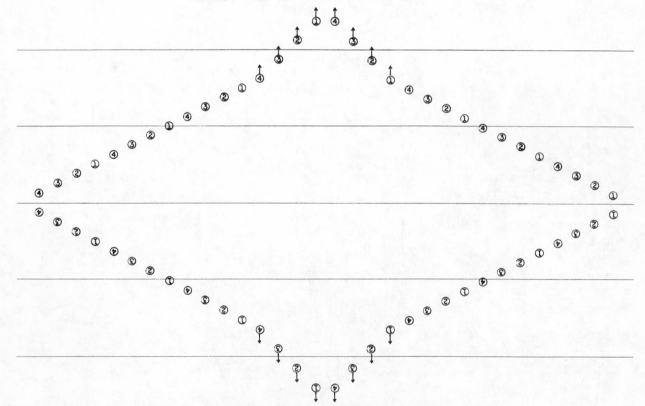

FIGURE 374—The movement continues.

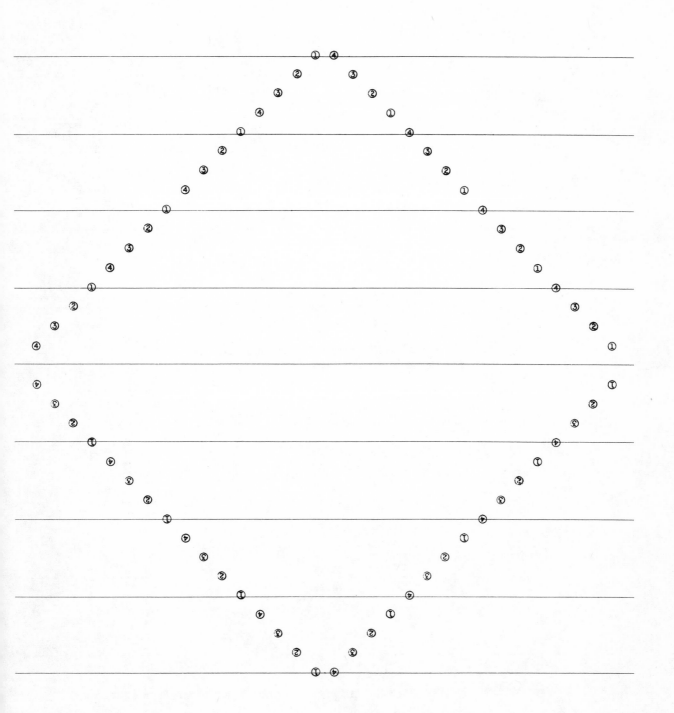

FIGURE 375—The movement is complete.

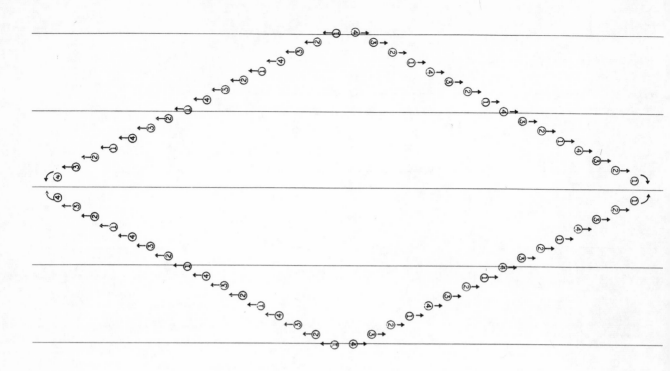

FIGURE 376—The diamond splits and each section moves to the side executing flank 2.

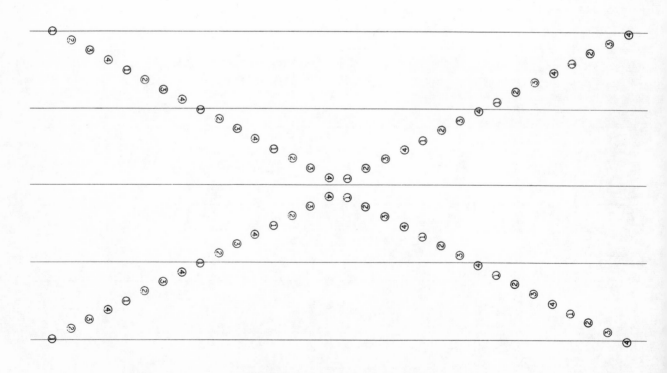

FIGURE 377—The movement is complete.

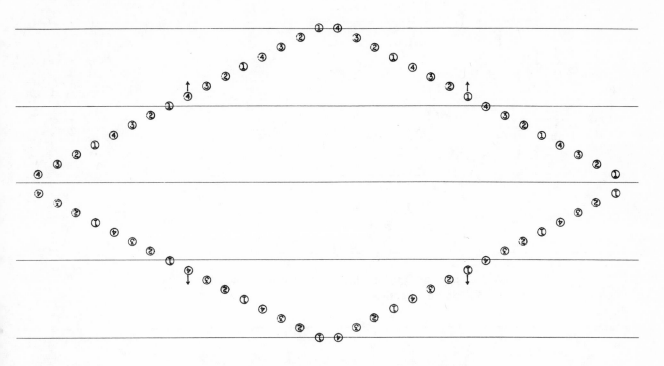

FIGURE 378—Each side executes step 2 from the center.

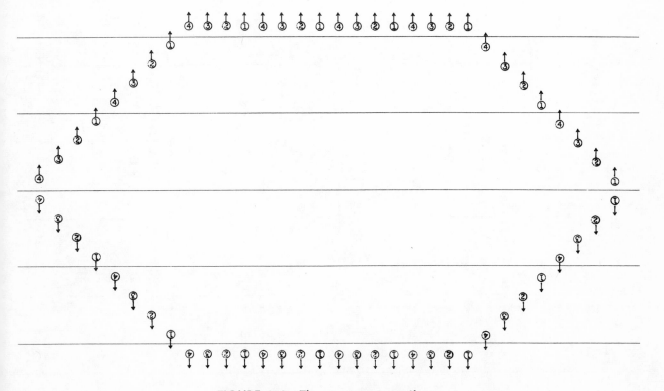

FIGURE 379—The movement continues.

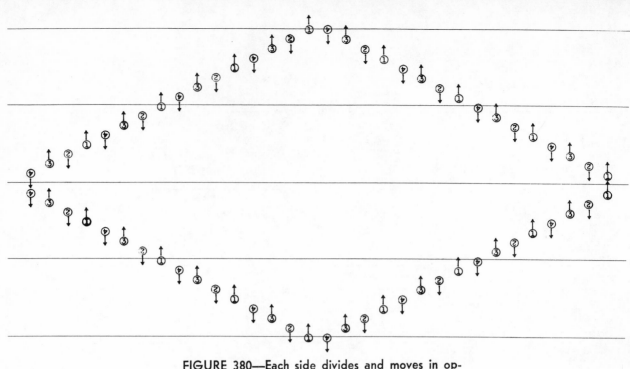

FIGURE 380—Each side divides and moves in opposite directions.

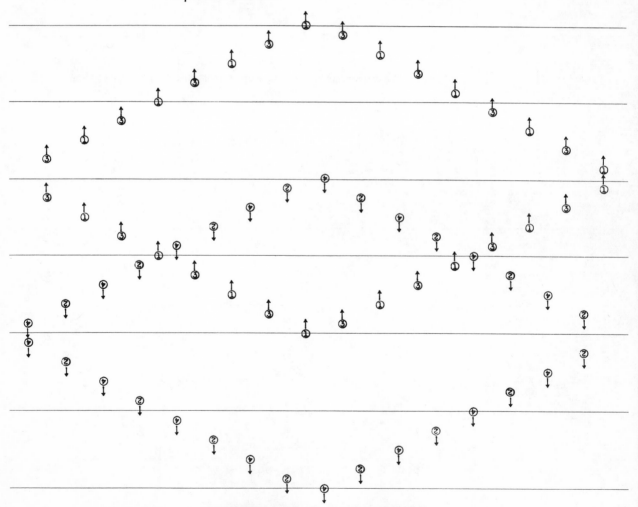

FIGURE 381—The movement continues.

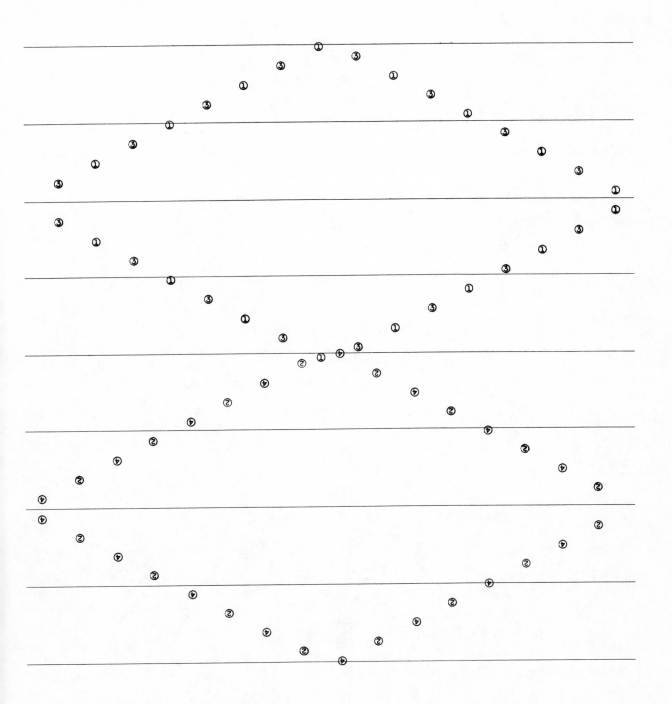

FIGURE 382—The movement is complete.

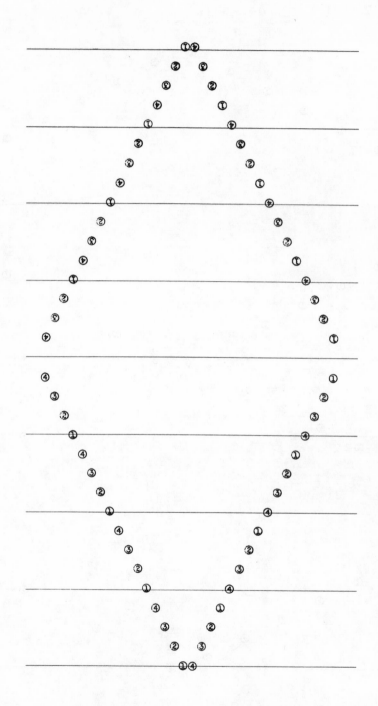

FIGURE 383—The above formation can be used for the preceding drill movements.

The Octo

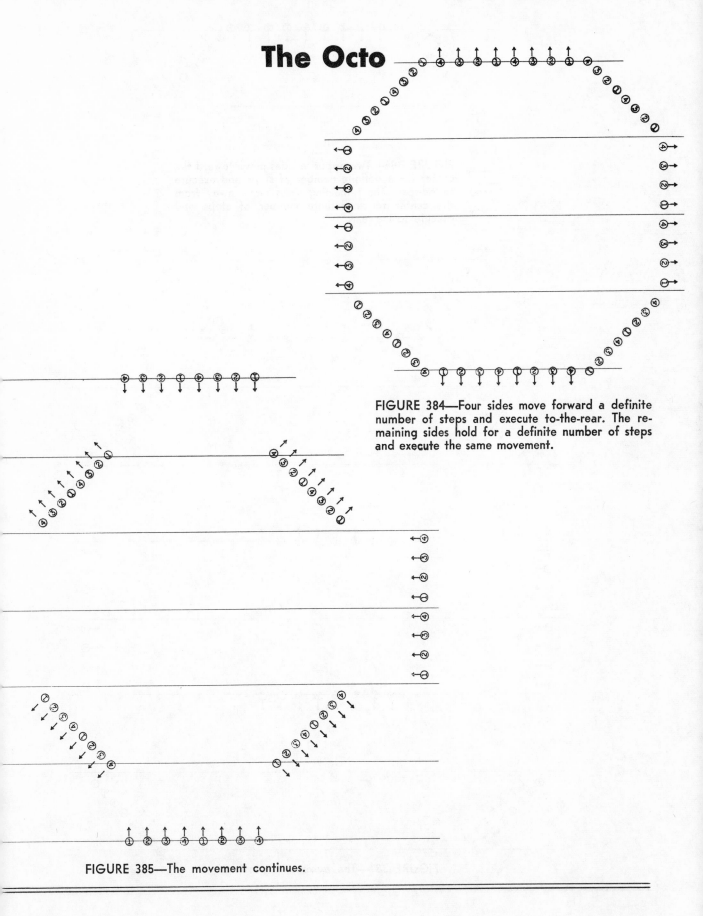

FIGURE 384—Four sides move forward a definite number of steps and execute to-the-rear. The remaining sides hold for a definite number of steps and execute the same movement.

FIGURE 385—The movement continues.

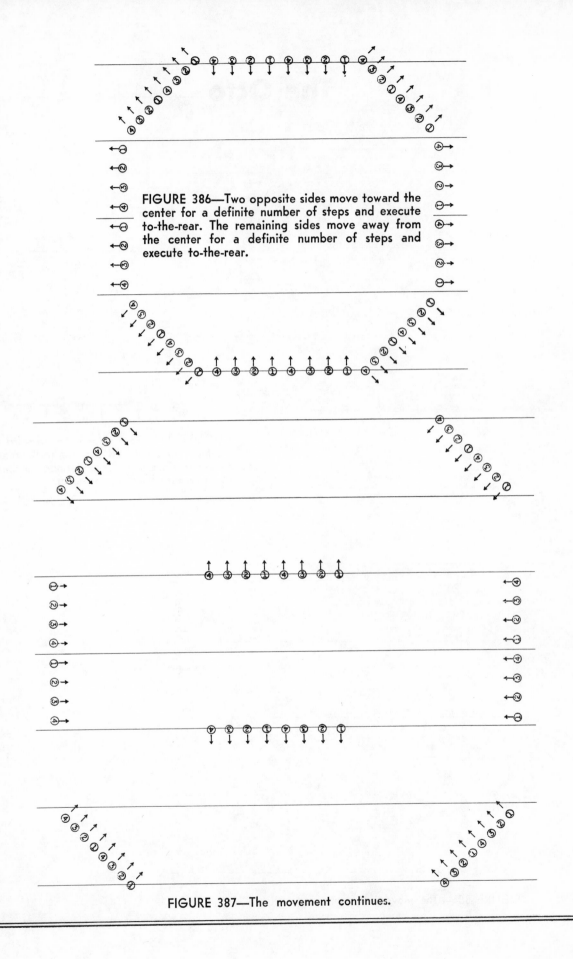

FIGURE 386—Two opposite sides move toward the center for a definite number of steps and execute to-the-rear. The remaining sides move away from the center for a definite number of steps and execute to-the-rear.

FIGURE 387—The movement continues.

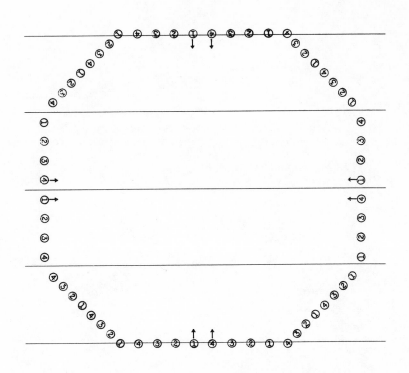

FIGURE 388—Four opposite sides execute step 2.

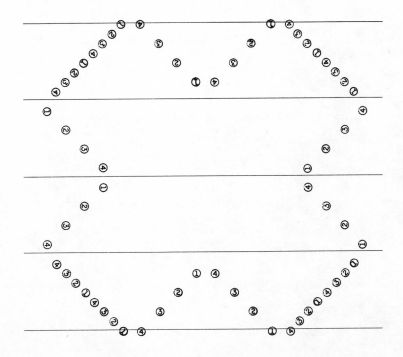

FIGURE 389—The movement is complete.

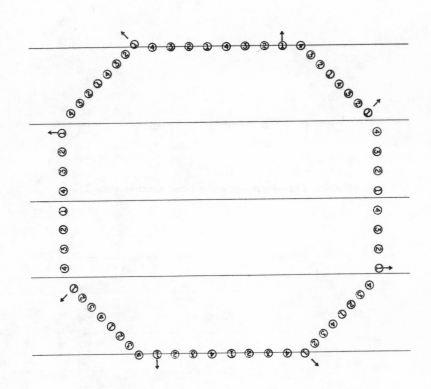

FIGURE 390—Each side executes step 2 from the right.

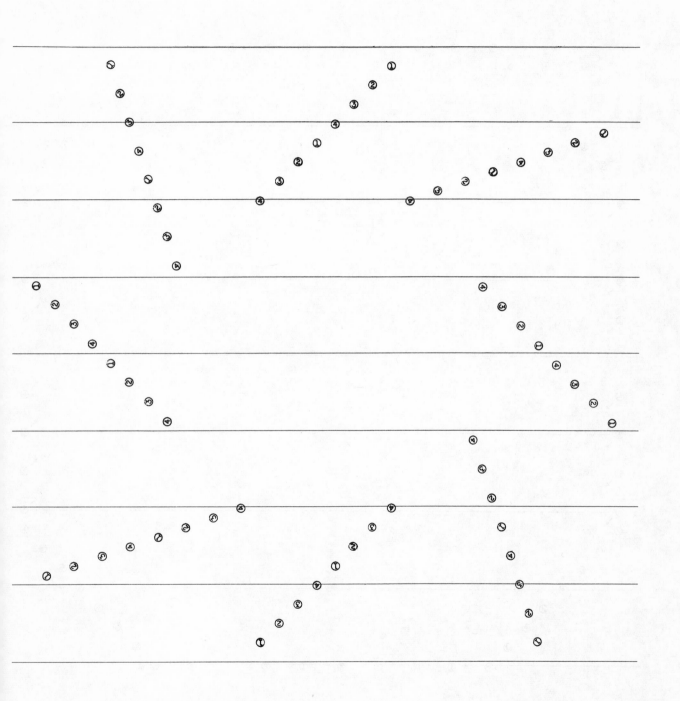

FIGURE 391—The movement is complete. The unit
is in position for silent drill.

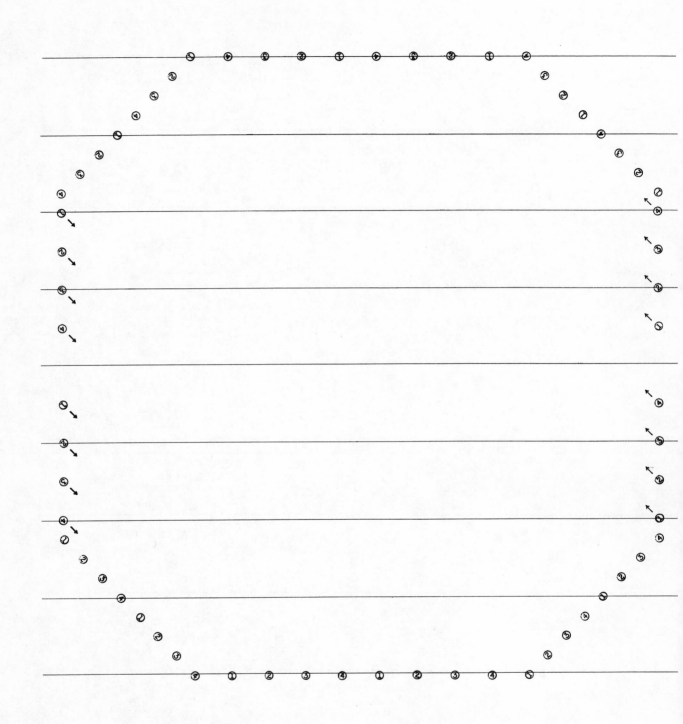

FIGURE 392—Two opposite sides oblique and fill
in with other sides.

FIGURE 393—The movement is complete.

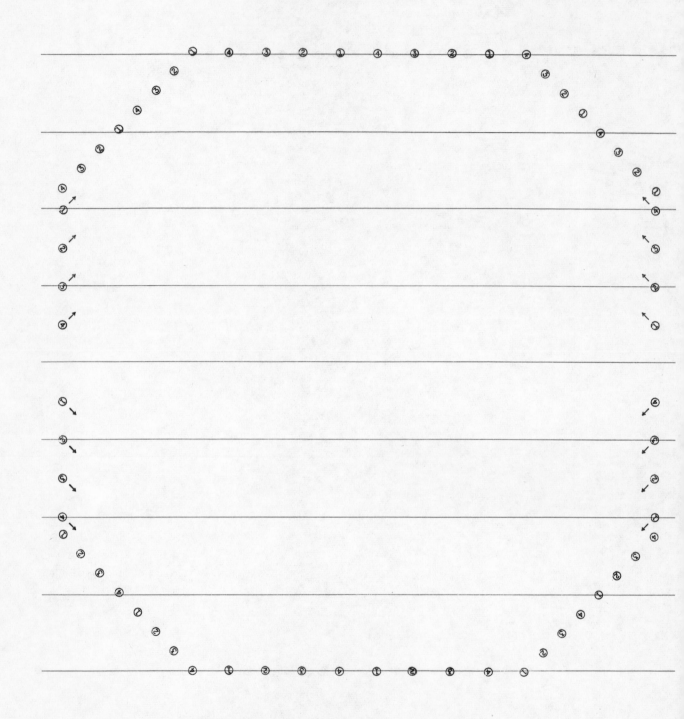

FIGURE 394—Two opposite sides split and oblique
and fill in other sides.

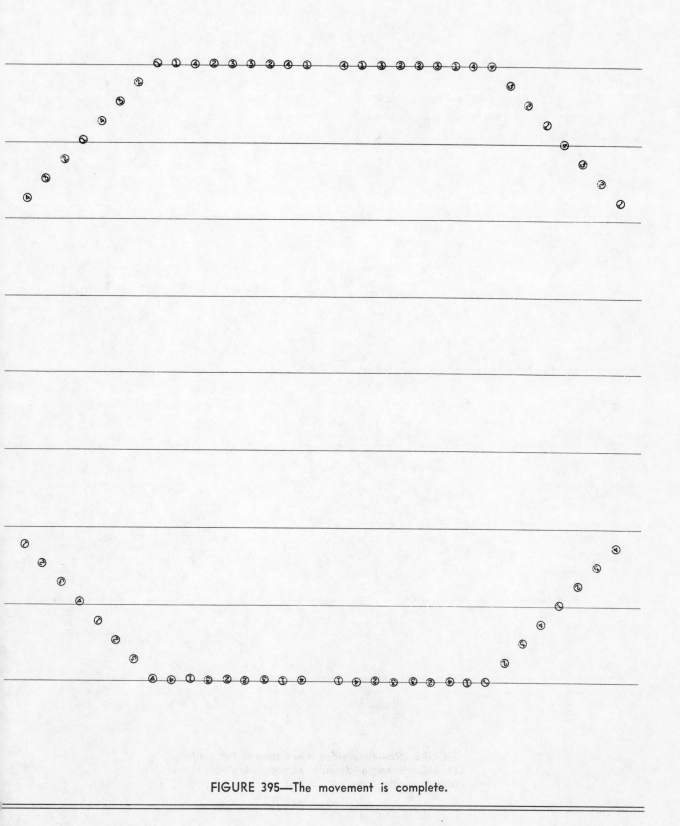

FIGURE 395—The movement is complete.

FIGURE 396—Four sides move toward the center
at oblique for a definite number of steps and
execute to-the-rear.

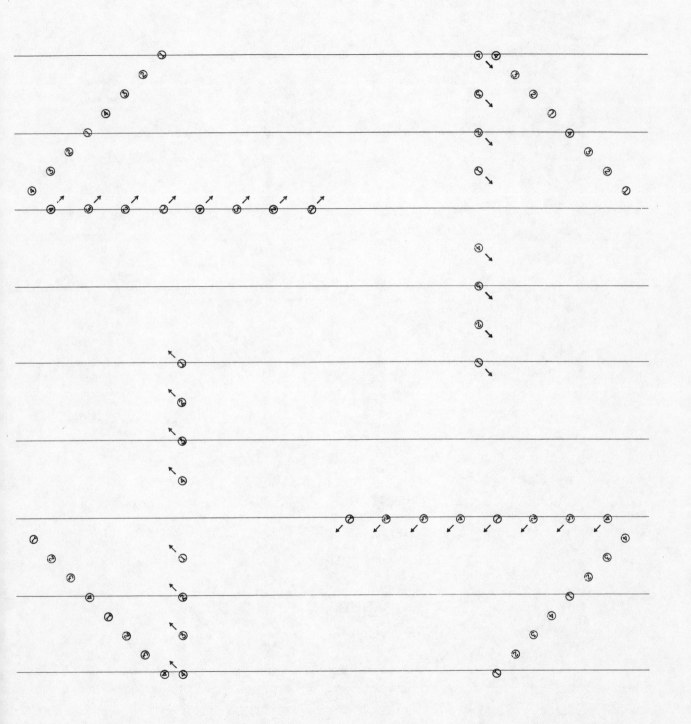

FIGURE 397—The movement continues.

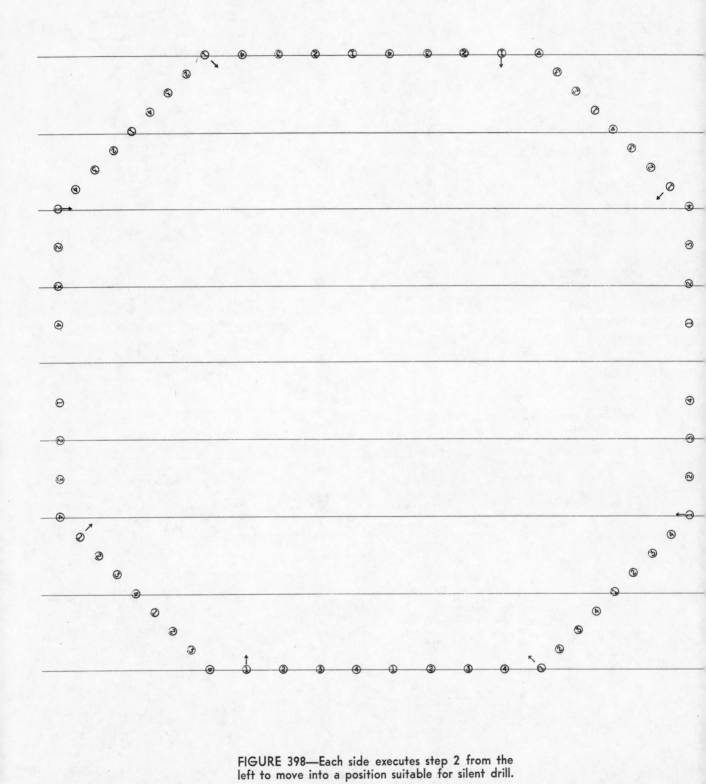

FIGURE 398—Each side executes step 2 from the
left to move into a position suitable for silent drill.

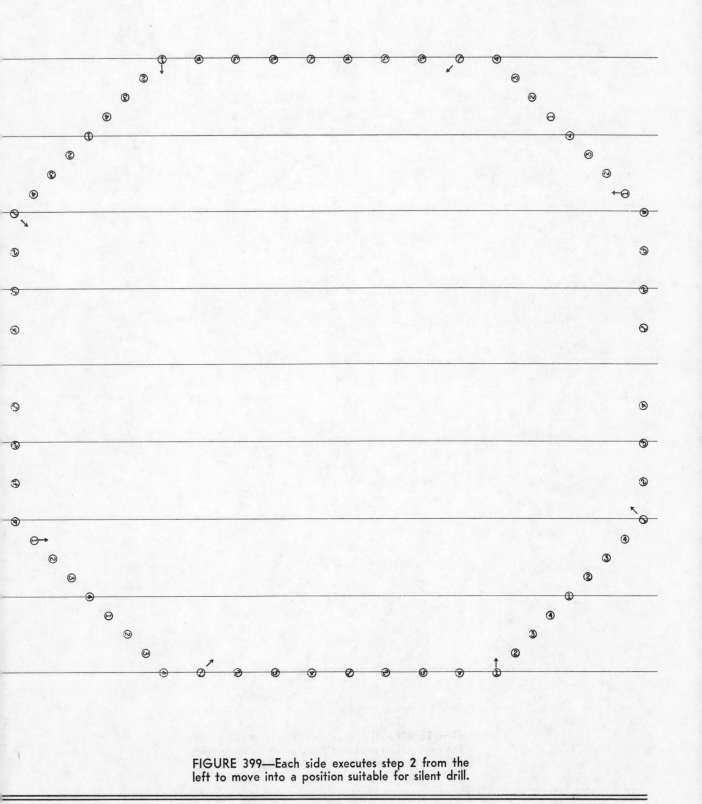

FIGURE 399—Each side executes step 2 from the
left to move into a position suitable for silent drill.

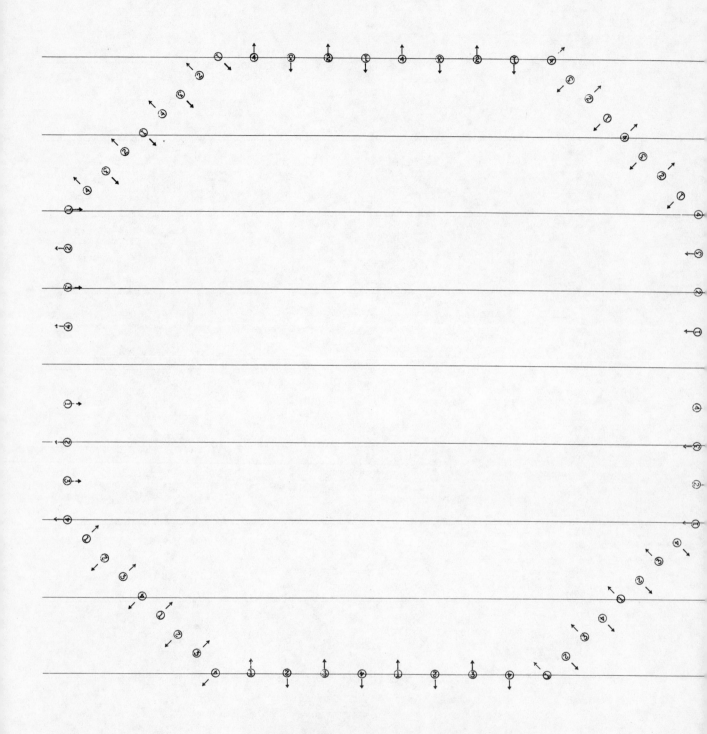

FIGURE 400—The ones and threes move toward the center. The twos and fours move to the outside. After a definite number of steps the unit executes to-the-rear.

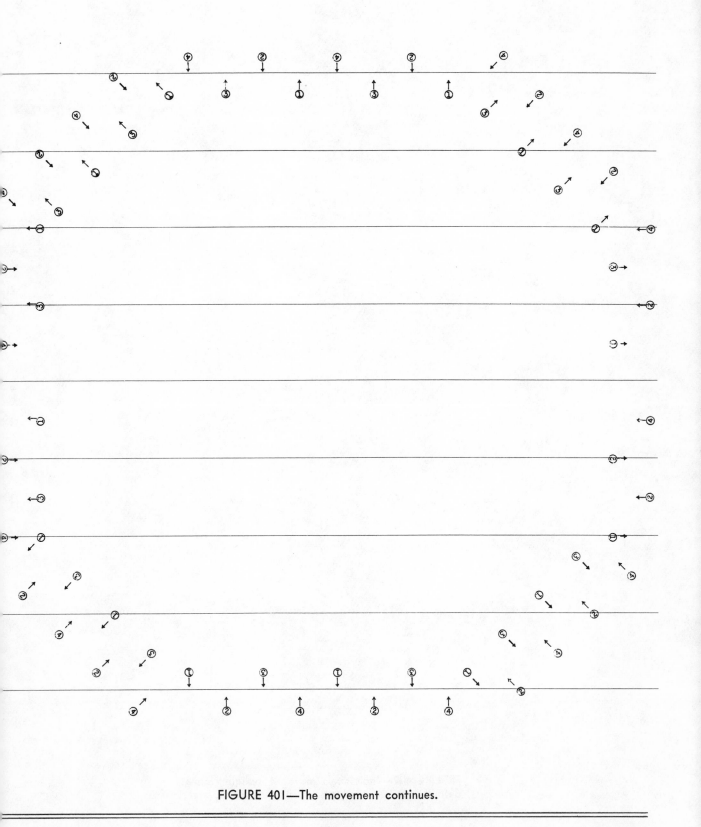

FIGURE 401—The movement continues.

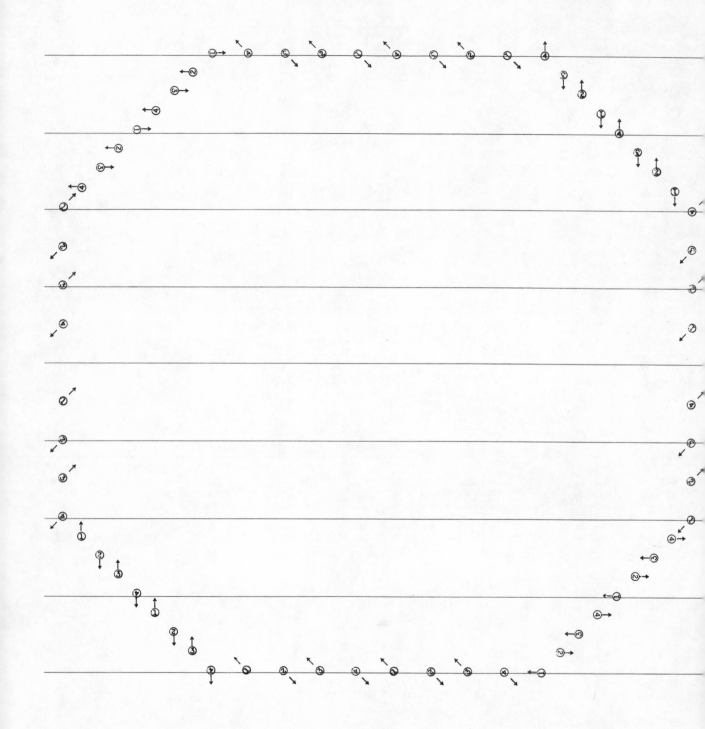

FIGURE 402—Individuals move at oblique for a
definite number of steps and execute to-the-rear.

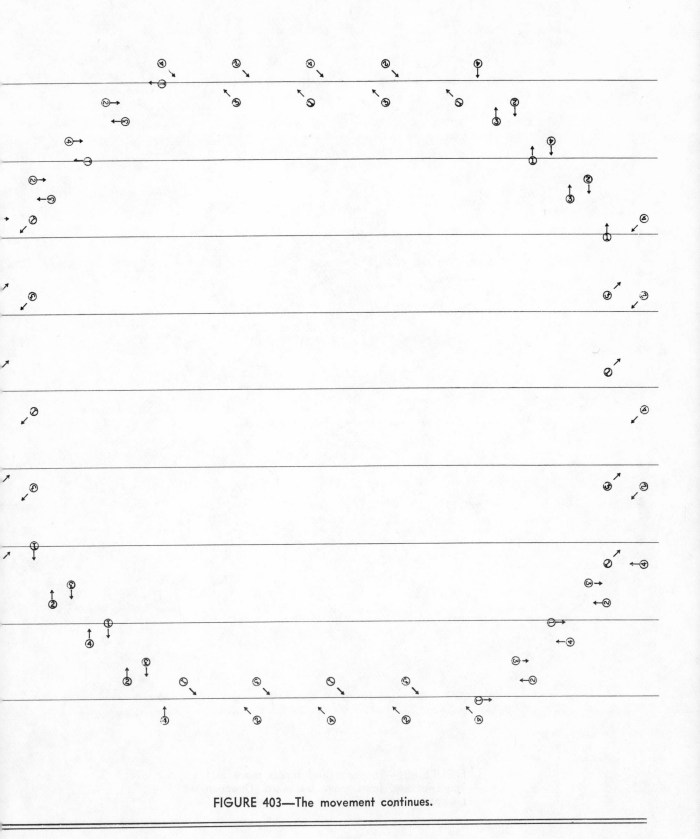

FIGURE 403—The movement continues.

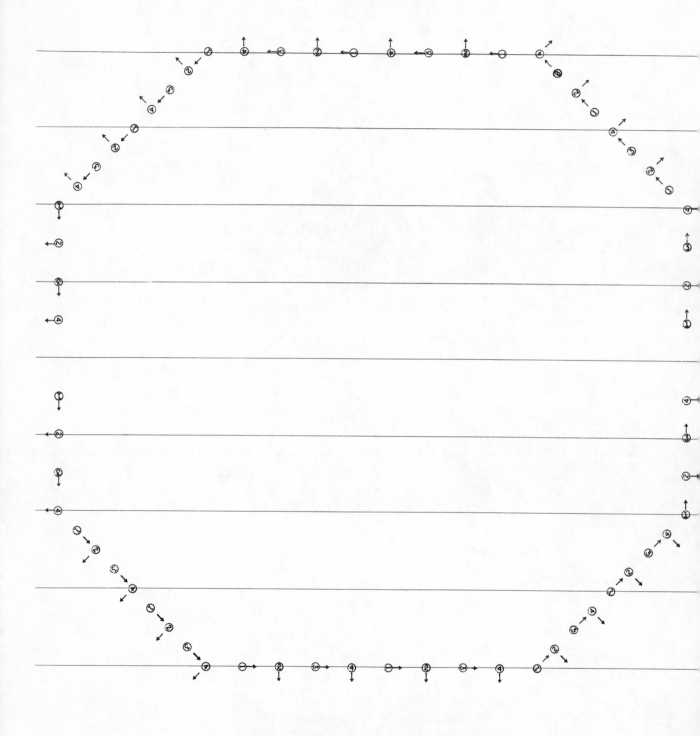

FIGURE 404—The ones and threes move in file. The twos and fours move backward. Direction is changed after a definite number of steps.

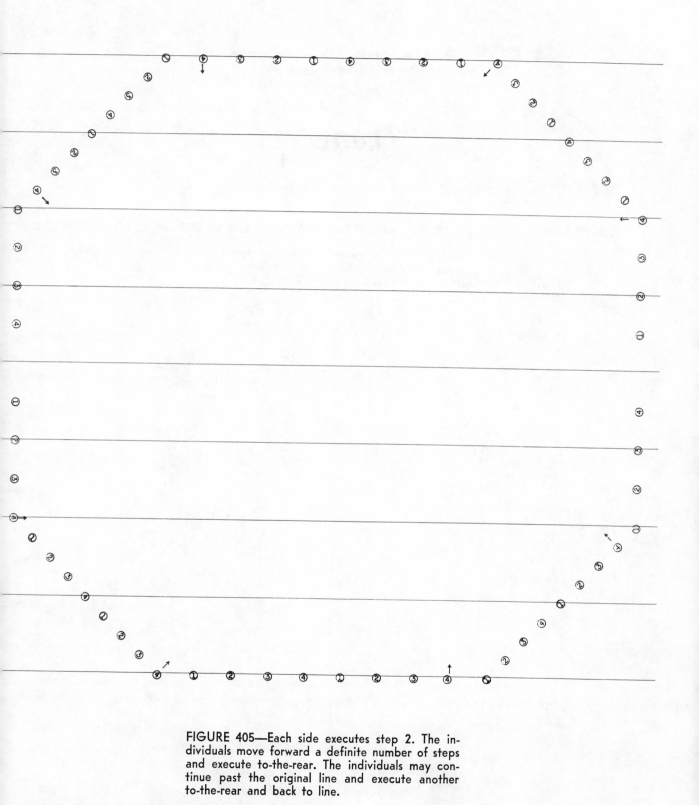

FIGURE 405—Each side executes step 2. The individuals move forward a definite number of steps and execute to-the-rear. The individuals may continue past the original line and execute another to-the-rear and back to line.

Circles

The drill movements of the squares and the octo are adaptable for the circle.

Letters

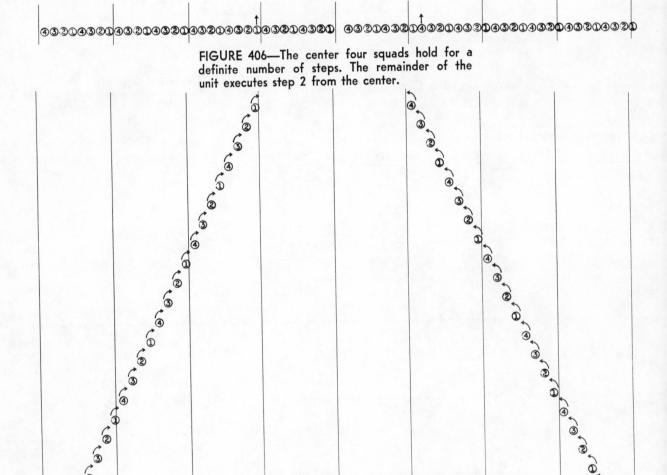

FIGURE 406—The center four squads hold for a definite number of steps. The remainder of the unit executes step 2 from the center.

FIGURE 407—The side elements flank toward the center. The four center squads move forward and spread.

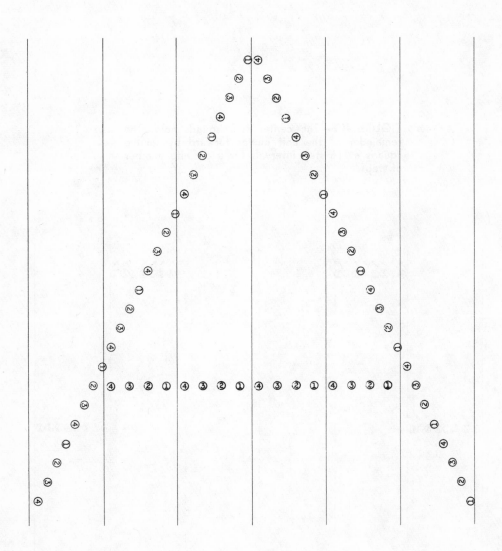

FIGURE 408—The letter is formed. The letter can
be changed to fit the perspective of the situation.

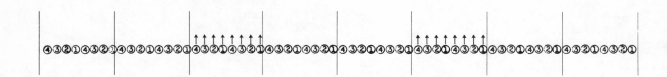

FIGURE 409—The center four squads hold. The remainder of the unit moves forward by double squads at 16 step intervals for a definite number of steps.

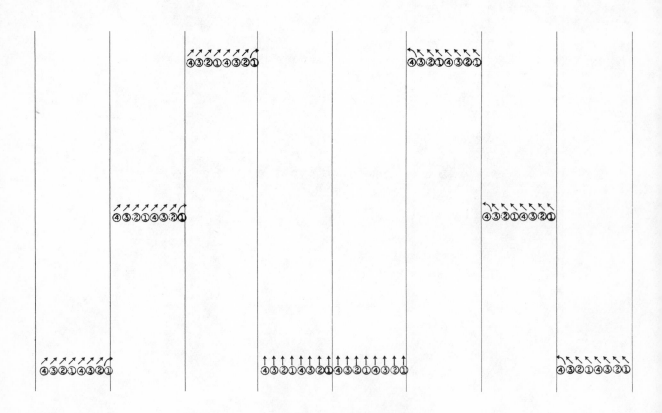

FIGURE 410—The center four squads move forward and spread as they move. The double squads wheel 135 degrees to the inside. The double squads open as they turn the last 45 degrees.

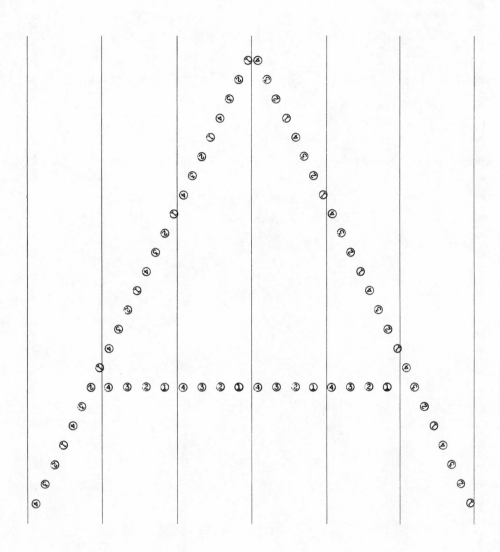

FIGURE 411—The movement is complete.

FIGURE 412—Each row executes a peel.

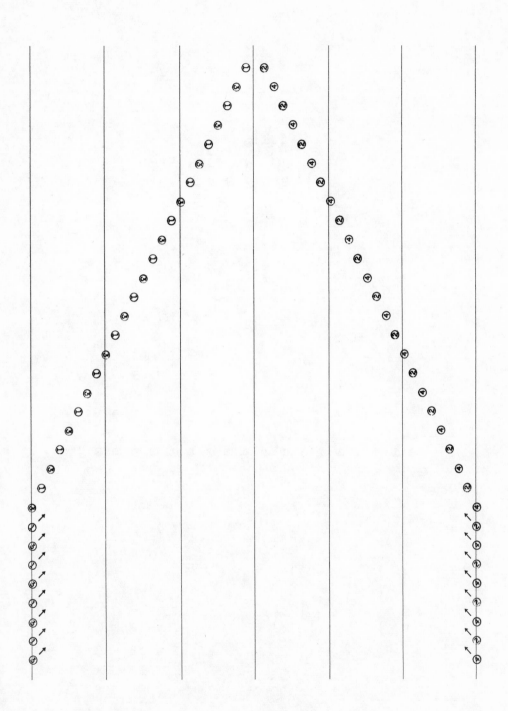

FIGURE 413—The ends of each row oblique to
position to form the cross bar.

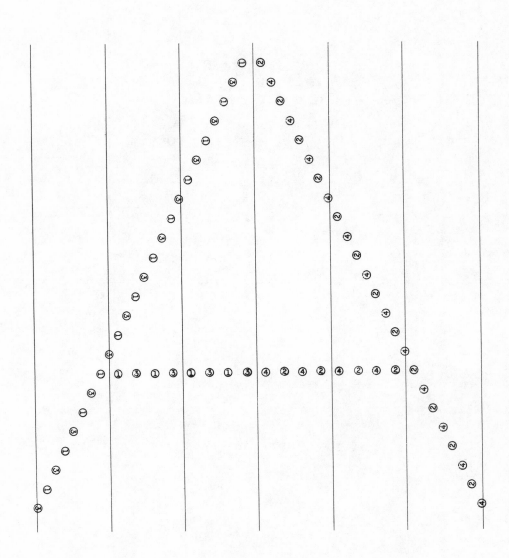

FIGURE 414—The letter is formed.

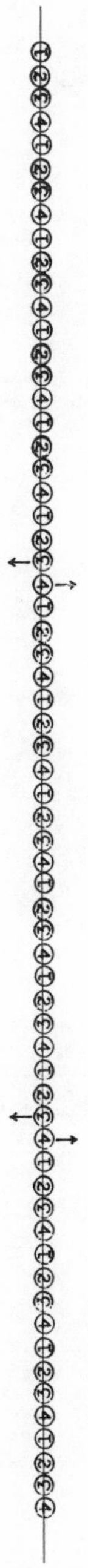

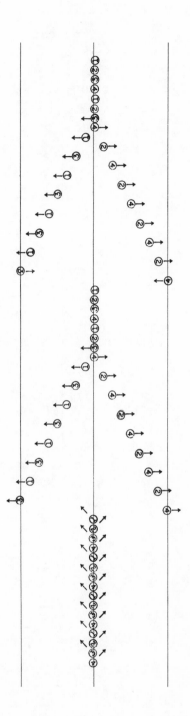

FIGURE 415—The line is divided into three sections. The lower section holds for a definite number of steps. The other sections peel from the lower side.

FIGURE 416—The lower section obliques to position. The top section executes to-the-rear by individuals.

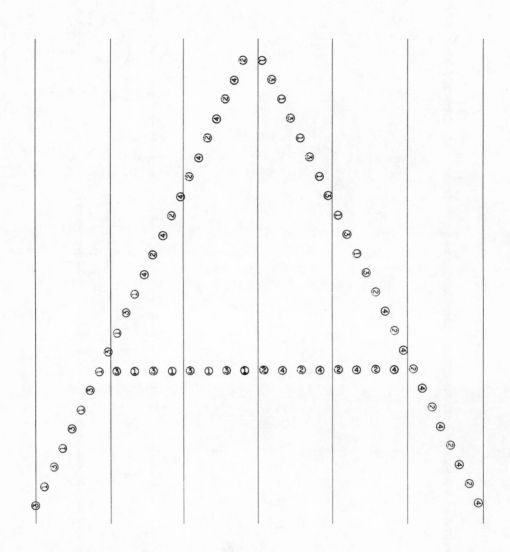

FIGURE 417—The letter is formed.

FIGURE 418—The unit is divided into three sections. The center section holds. The other sections execute step 2.

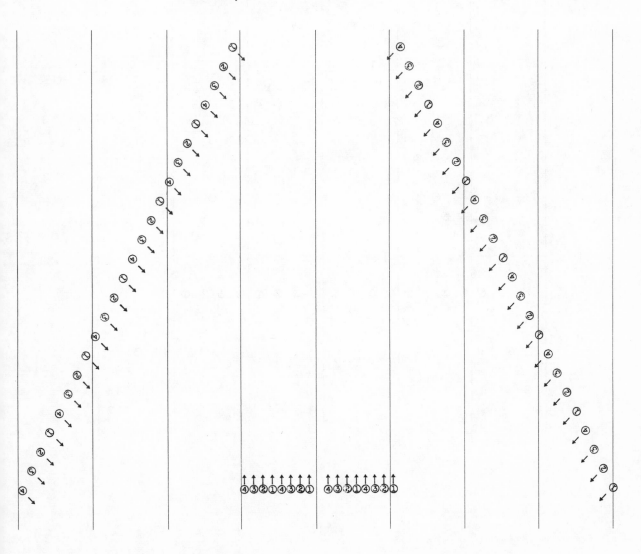

FIGURE 419—The center section moves forward and opens as it moves into position. The other sections oblique into position.

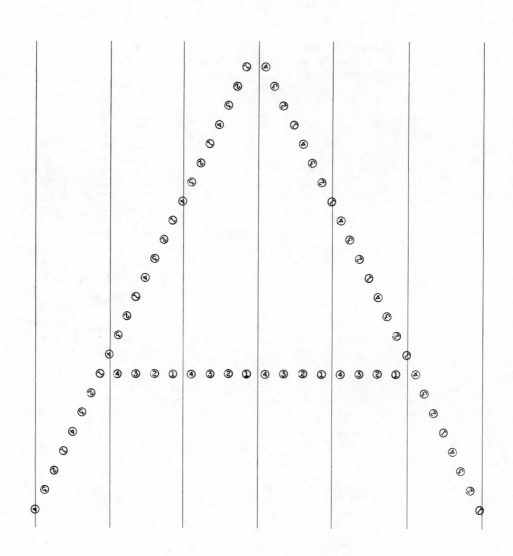

FIGURE 420—The letter is complete.

FIGURE 421—The unit is divided into three sections. The center section executes step 2 from the center. The outside sections execute step 2 and side step to set up a point of departure.

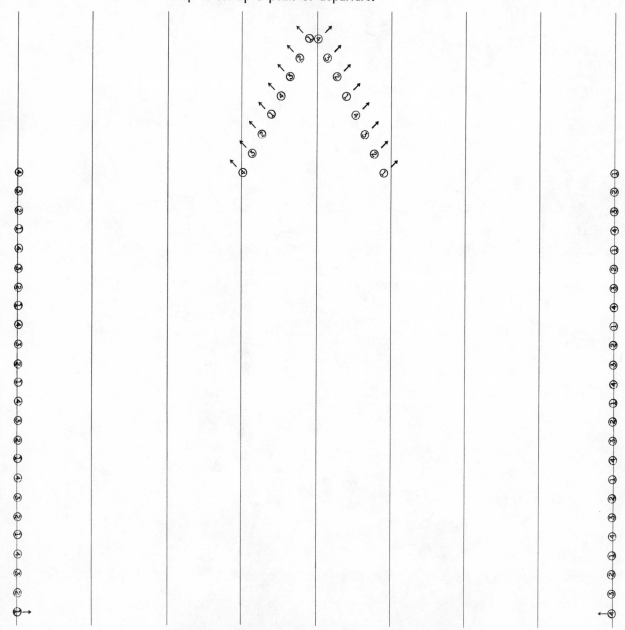

FIGURE 422—The center section executes silent drill. The outside sections turn toward the center and execute step 2.

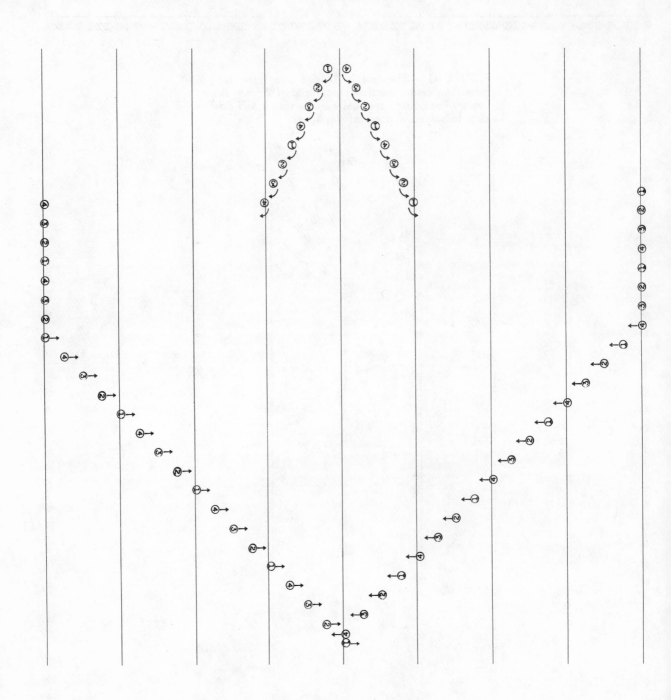

FIGURE 423—The outside sections move through
each other and move into position.

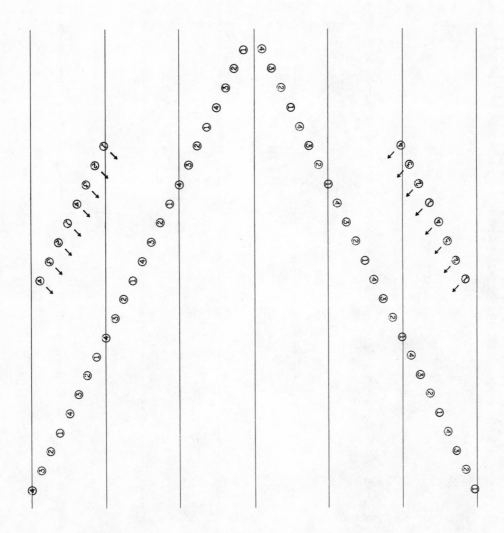

FIGURE 424—The outside sections are now in position. The center section obliques into position.

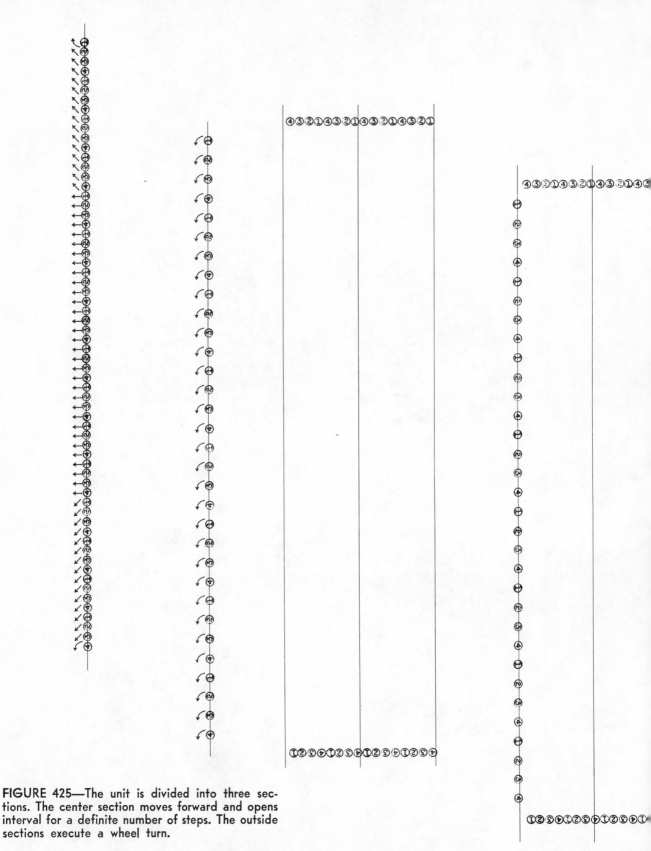

FIGURE 425—The unit is divided into three sections. The center section moves forward and opens interval for a definite number of steps. The outside sections execute a wheel turn.

FIGURE 426—The movement continues.

FIGURE 427—The movement is complete.

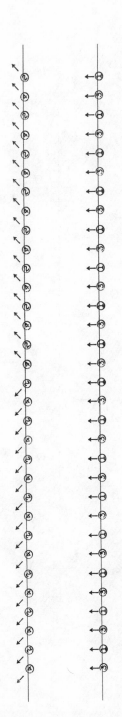

FIGURE 428—The leading row splits and obliques
to line.

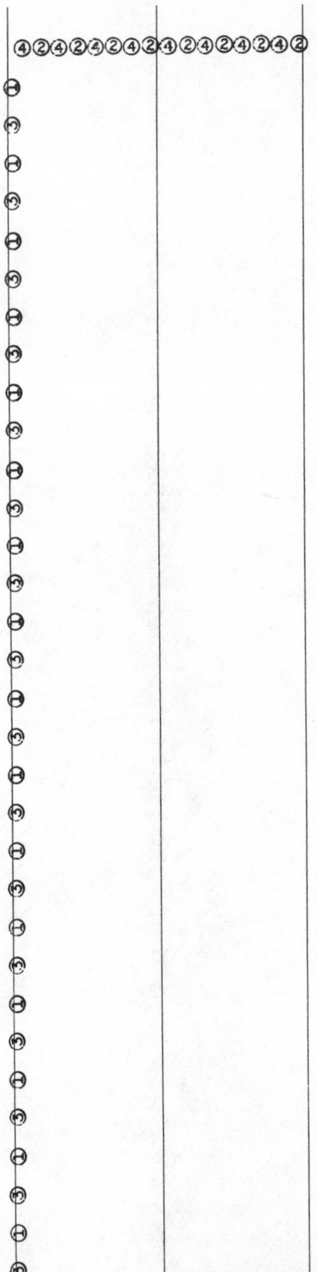

FIGURE 429—The movement is complete.

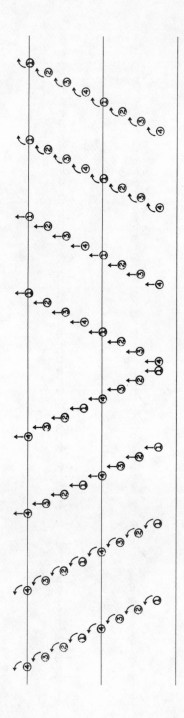

FIGURE 430—Each double squad executes step 2.

FIGURE 431—Two outside double squads flank to the outside and mesh to form top and bottom of the "C." The remaining squads continue forward a definite number of steps and execute to-the-rear and open as they move on line.

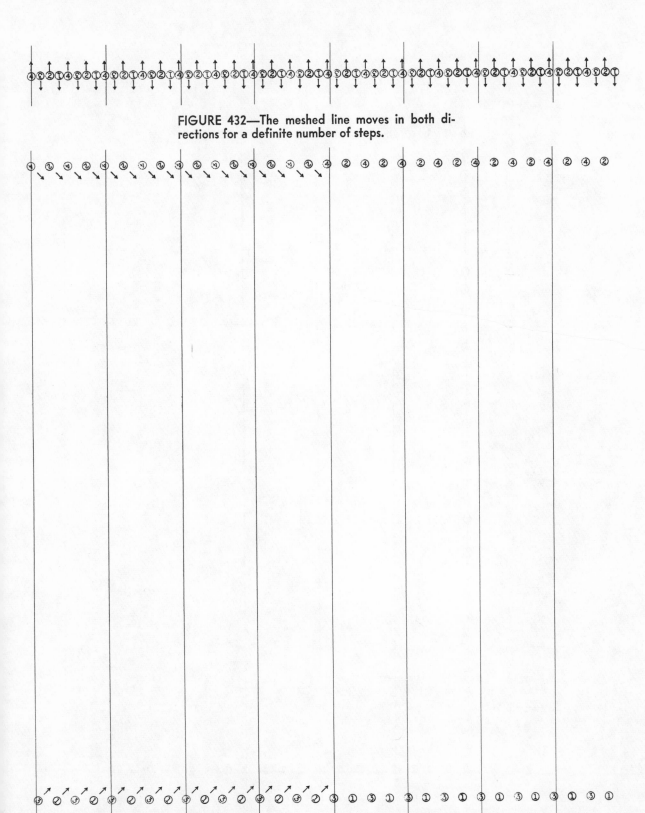

FIGURE 432—The meshed line moves in both directions for a definite number of steps.

FIGURE 433—Each row is split. Ones section of
each row holds. The remaining section obliques to
line.

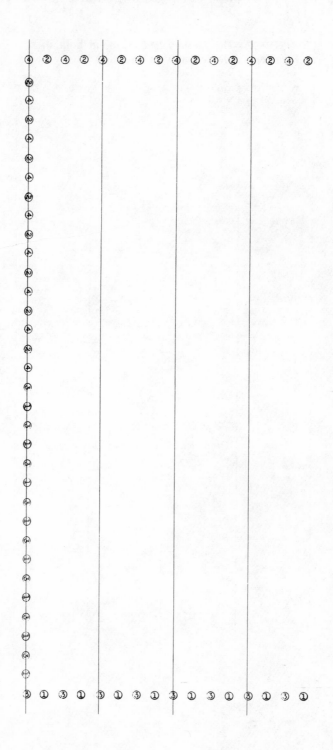

FIGURE 434—The movement is complete.

FIGURE 435—The unit is moving forward and executes halt 2 from both ends.

FIGURE 436—As the unit moves forward it opens
from the center.

FIGURE 437—The movement is complete.

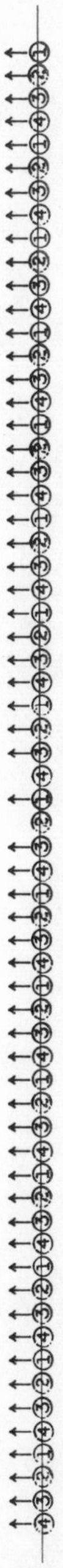

FIGURE 438—The unit is moving forward and executes halt 2 from the center. The individuals halt
for 2 steps and turn to the outside and move on line.

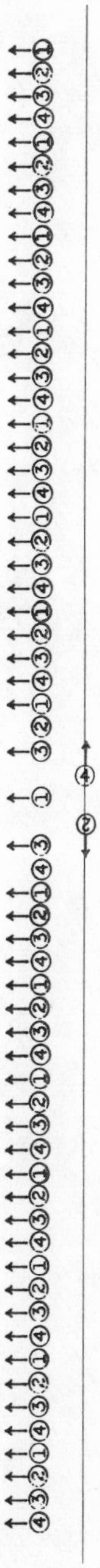

FIGURE 439—The movement continues.

FIGURE 440—The movement is complete.

FIGURE 441—The meshed line obliques to a new line.

FIGURE 442—The unit halts in place after a definite number of steps.

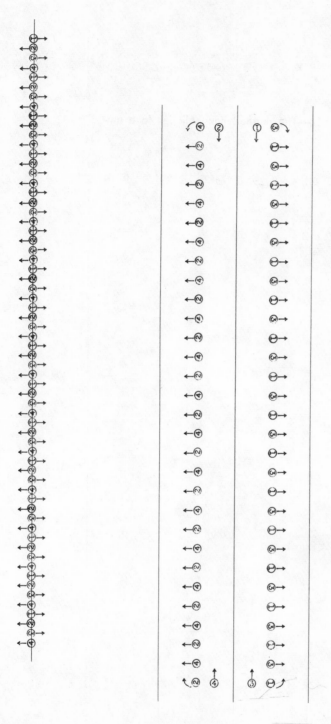

FIGURE 443—The meshed line moves in both directions and each row executes flank 2 from both ends.

FIGURE 444—The movement continues.

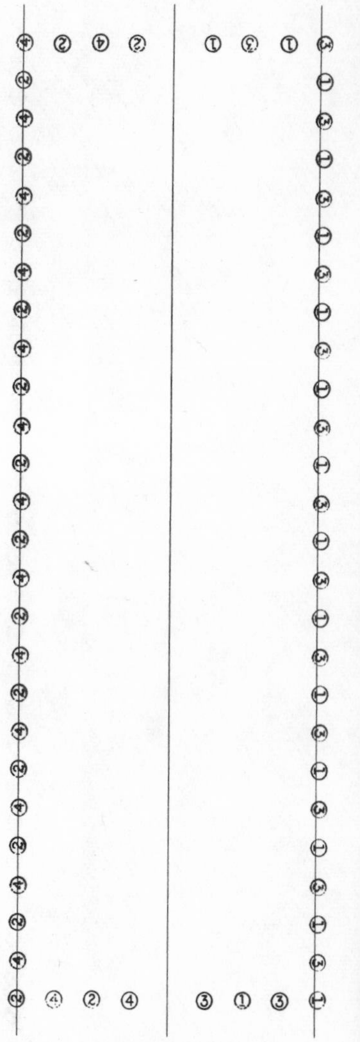

FIGURE 445—The movement is complete.

FIGURE 446—A double squad on each end turns and opens. The twos and fours move forward a definite number of steps.

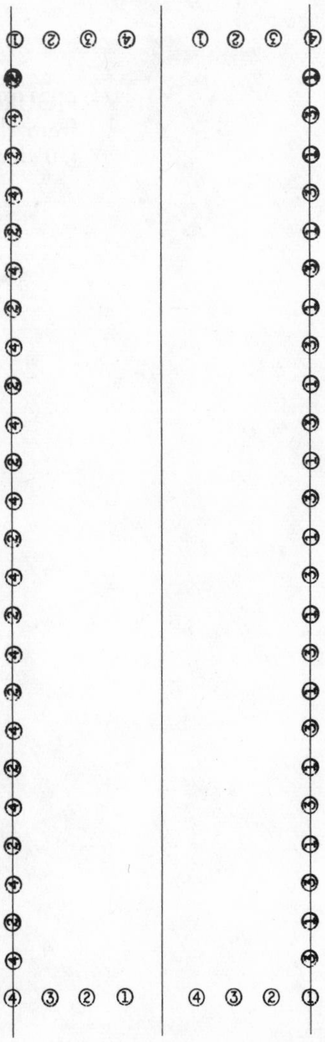

FIGURE 447—The movement is complete.

FIGURE 448—The twos and fours move forward
from the center section. The outside sections turn
(30 degrees) and oblique on to the new line.

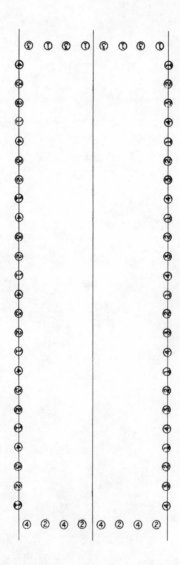

FIGURE 449—The movement is complete.

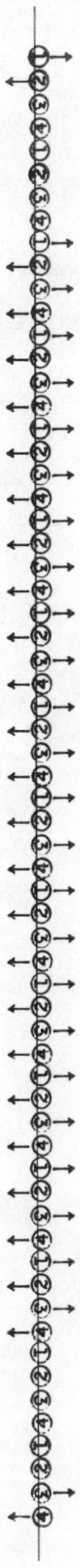

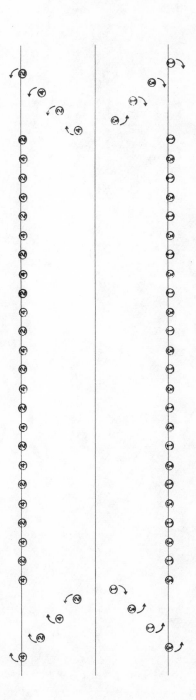

FIGURE 450—The center section moves in both directions. The end sections execute step 2.

FIGURE 451—The movement continues.

FIGURE 452—The twos and fours oblique on to a
new line. The ones and threes hold for a definite
number of steps and move forward.

FIGURE 453—The movement continues.

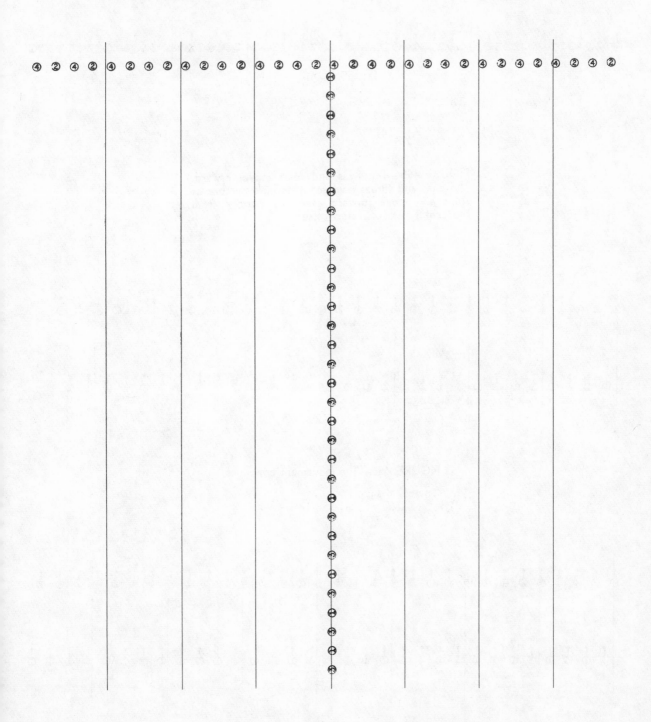

FIGURE 454—The movement is complete.

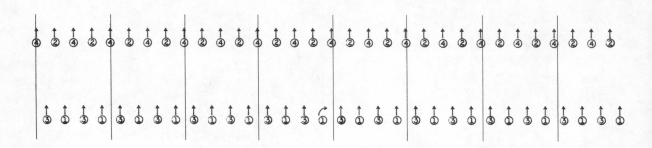

FIGURE 455—The twos and fours move forward. The ones and threes hold for a definite number of steps and move forward executing flank 4 from the center with a 2 step offset.

FIGURE 456—The movement continues.

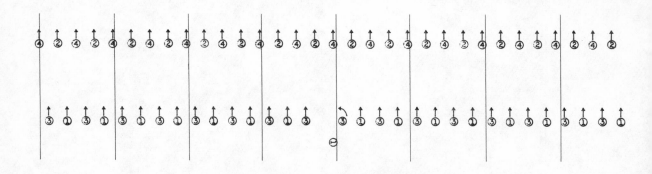

FIGURE 457—The movement continues.

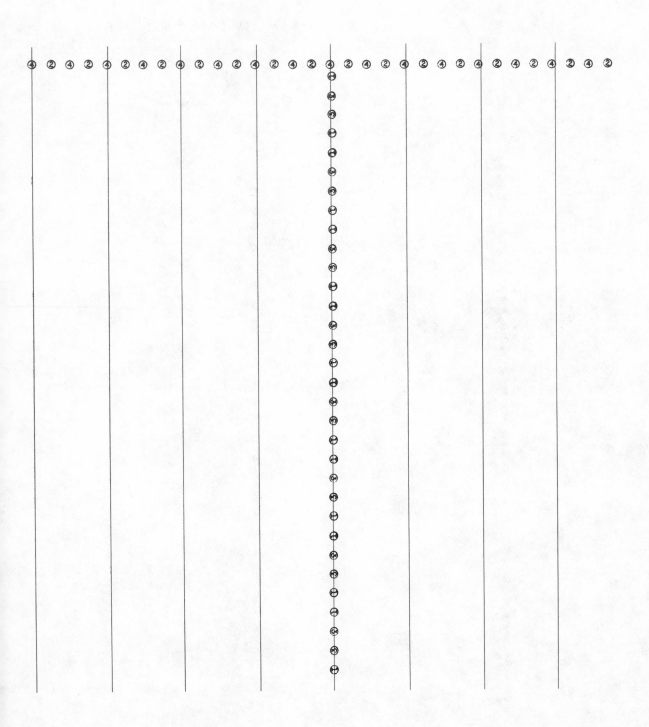

FIGURE 458—The movement is complete.

FIGURE 459—Ones and threes turn (60 degrees) and oblique on to a new line.

FIGURE 460—The movement is complete.

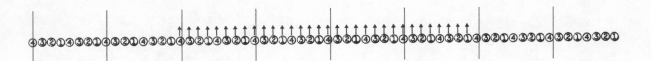

FIGURE 461—The center section moves forward.
The outside sections execute step 4.

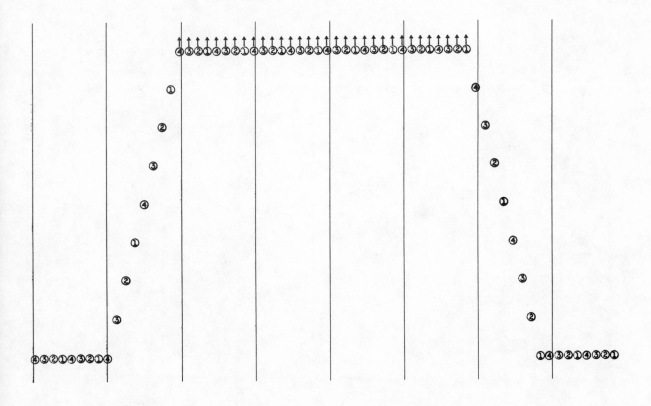

FIGURE 462—The movement continues.

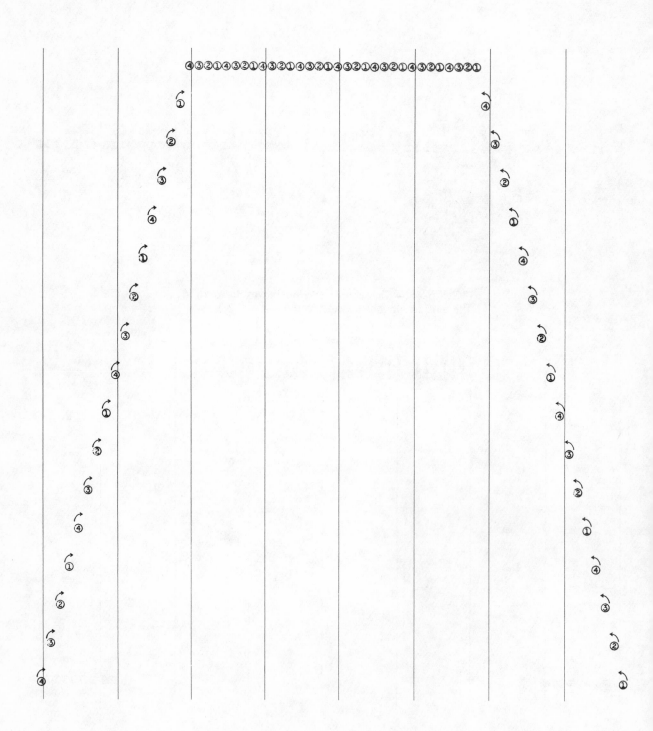

FIGURE 463—The outside sections turn toward the center and mesh on line.

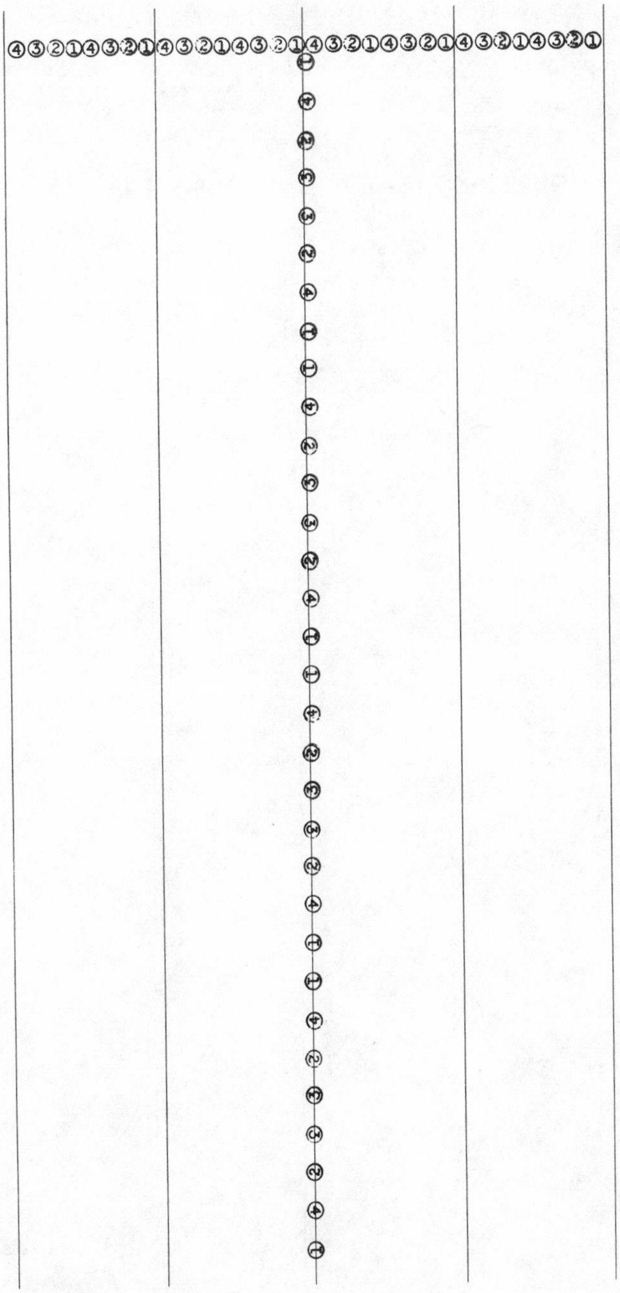

FIGURE 464—The movement is complete.

FIGURE 465—The unit executes step 4 from the
center and both ends.

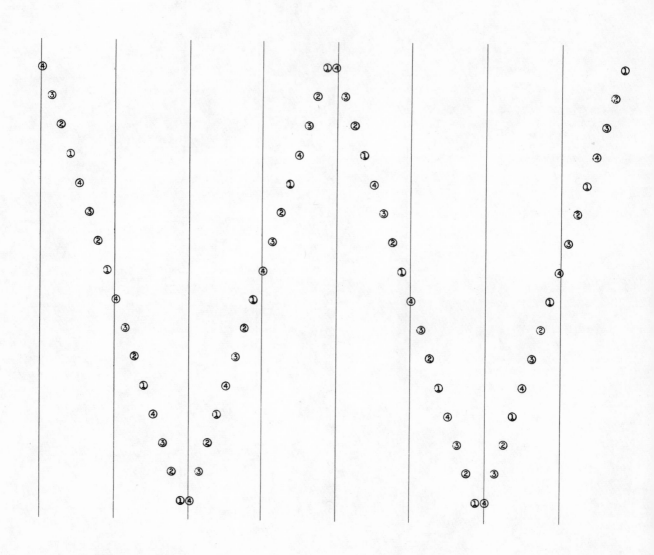

FIGURE 466—The movement is complete.

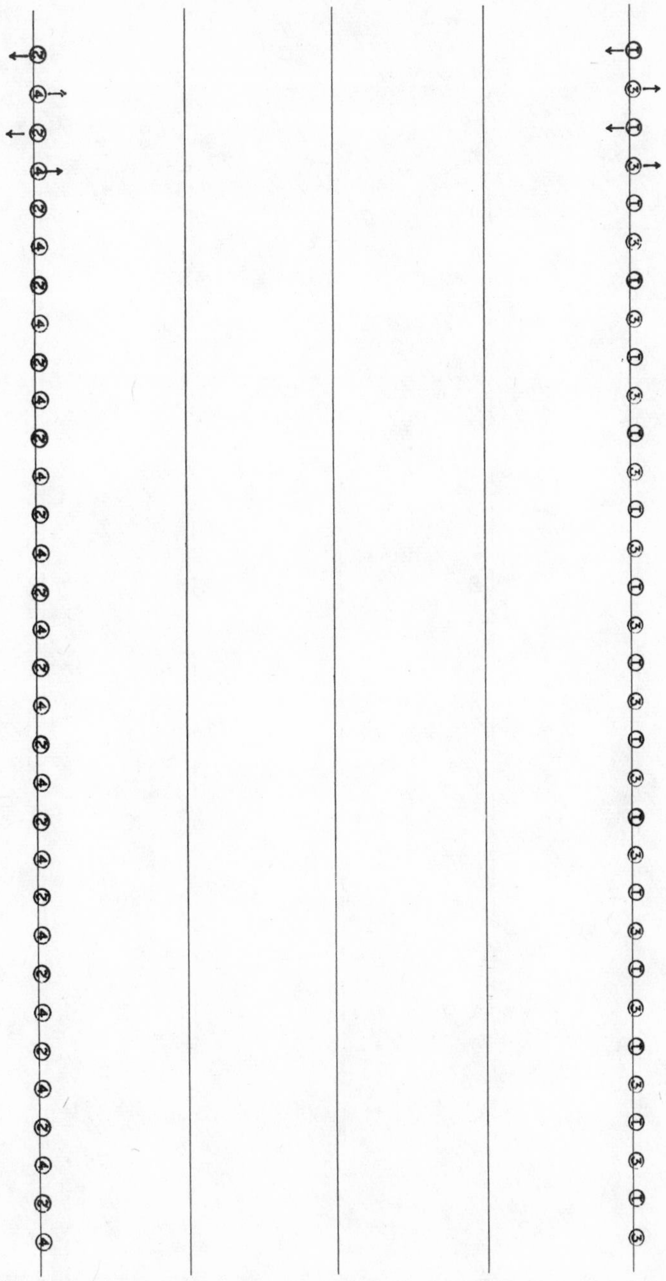

FIGURE 467—Each meshed line executes step 2.
Individuals move to position.

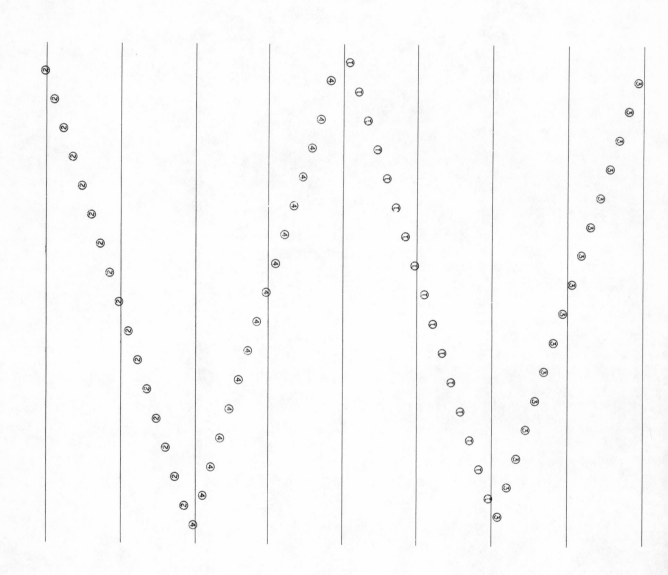

FIGURE 468—The movement is complete.

FIGURE 469—The unit executes step 2 from both ends.

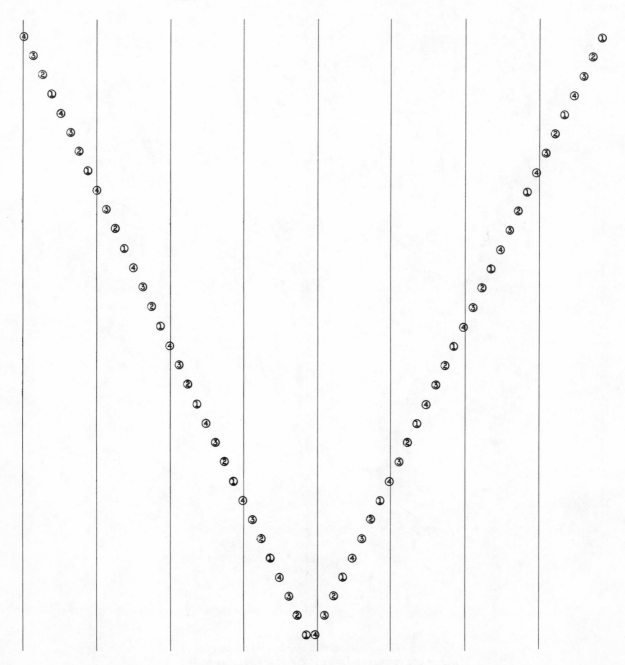

FIGURE 470—The movement is complete.

Exploding Letters

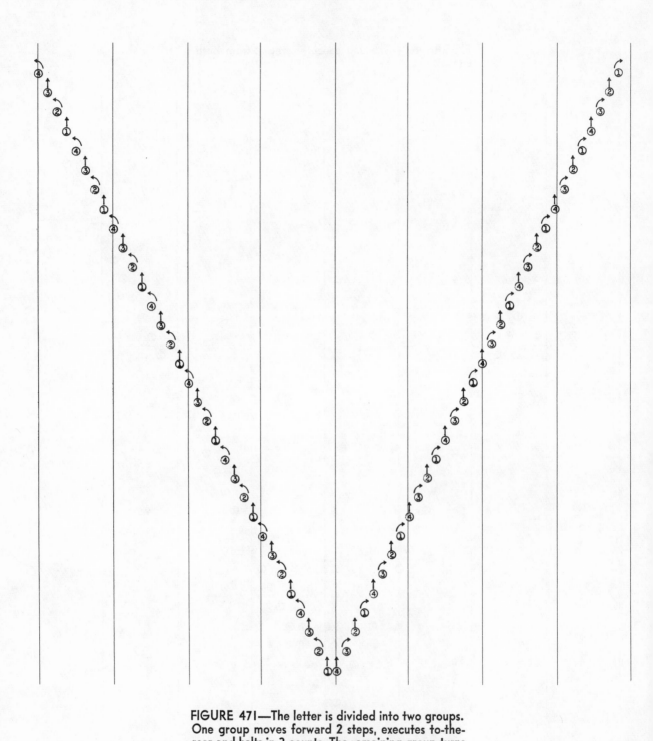

FIGURE 471—The letter is divided into two groups. One group moves forward 2 steps, executes to-the-rear and halts in 3 counts. The remaining group turns to the outside, moves 2 steps and executes a turn and halt.

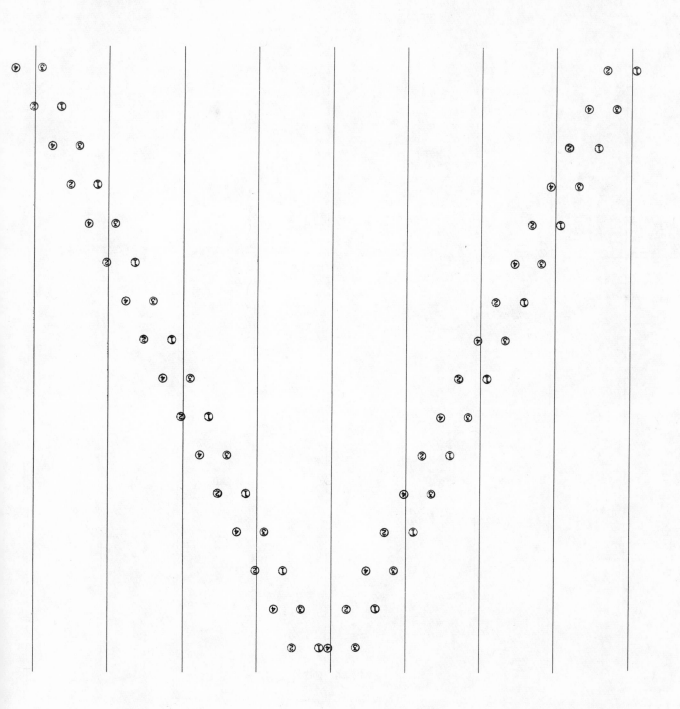

FIGURE 472—The movement is complete.

FIGURE 473—Each group of 2 turns to the outside,
moves one step, and executes a turn and halt.

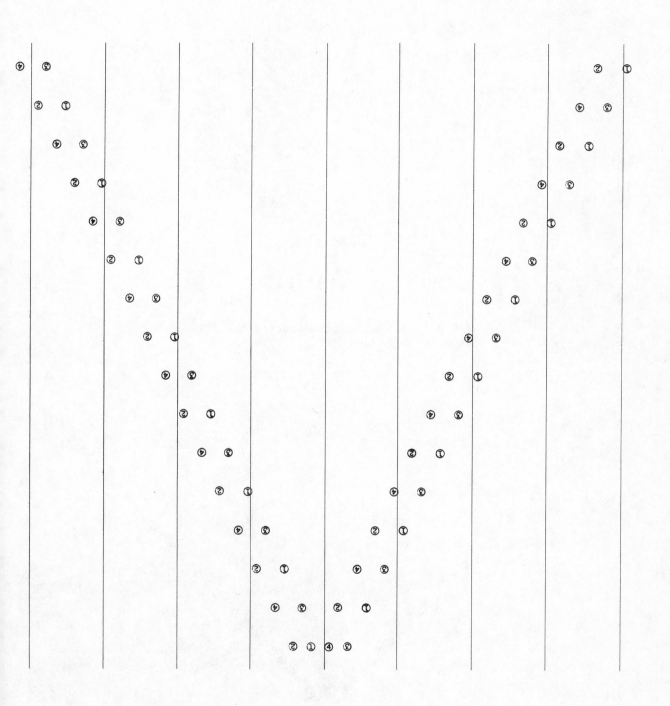

FIGURE 474—The movement is complete.

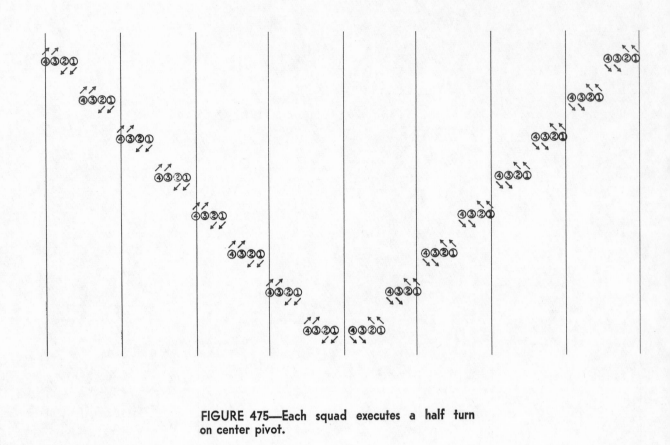

FIGURE 475—Each squad executes a half turn on center pivot.

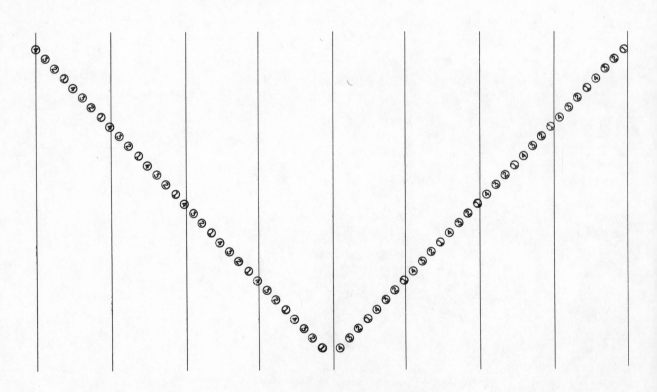

FIGURE 476—The movement is complete.

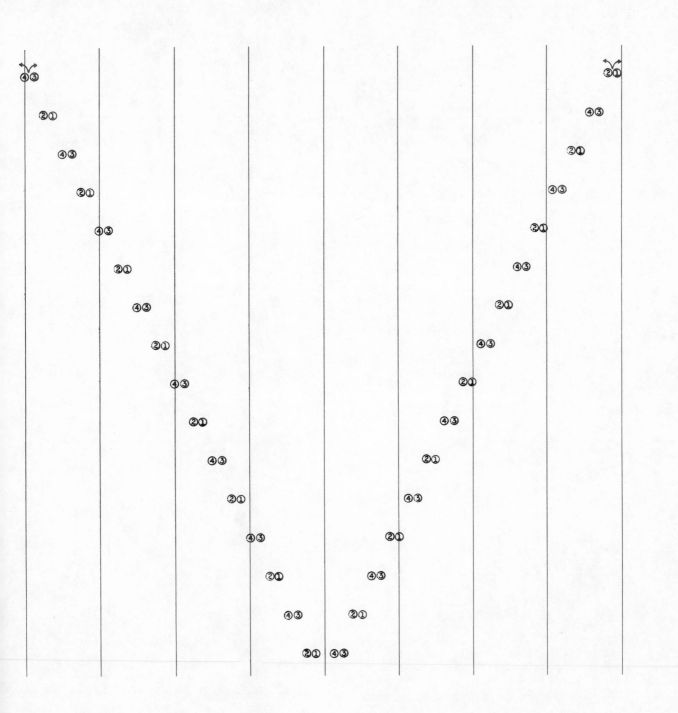

FIGURE 477—Each group of 2 explodes in order
starting with the top groups.

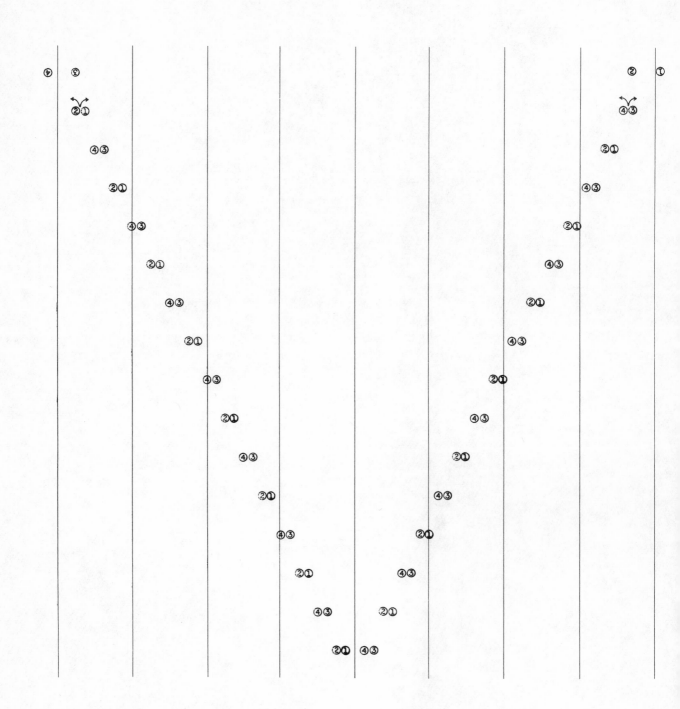

FIGURE 478—The movement continues.

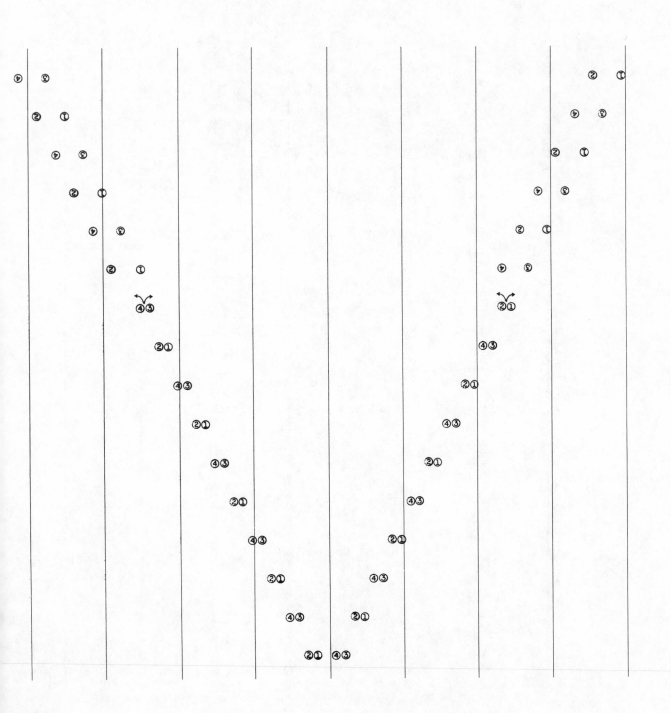

FIGURE 479—The movement continues.

Formations From Line

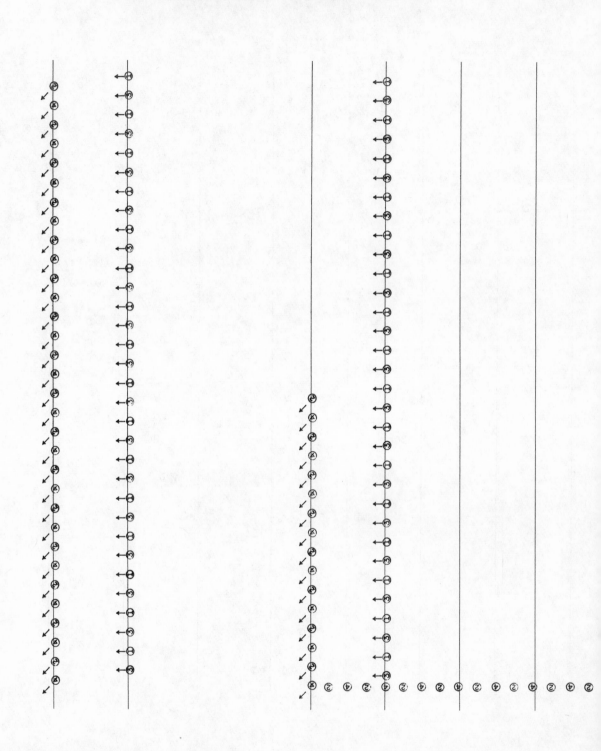

FIGURE 480—The leading row obliques on to a new line. The second row moves forward.

FIGURE 481—The movement continues.

FIGURE 482—The movement is complete.

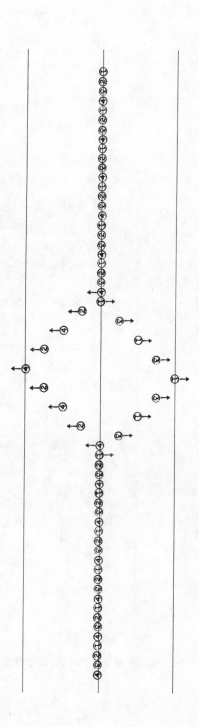

FIGURE 483—Each direction of the meshed line
executes step 2 from the center.

FIGURE 484—The movement continues.

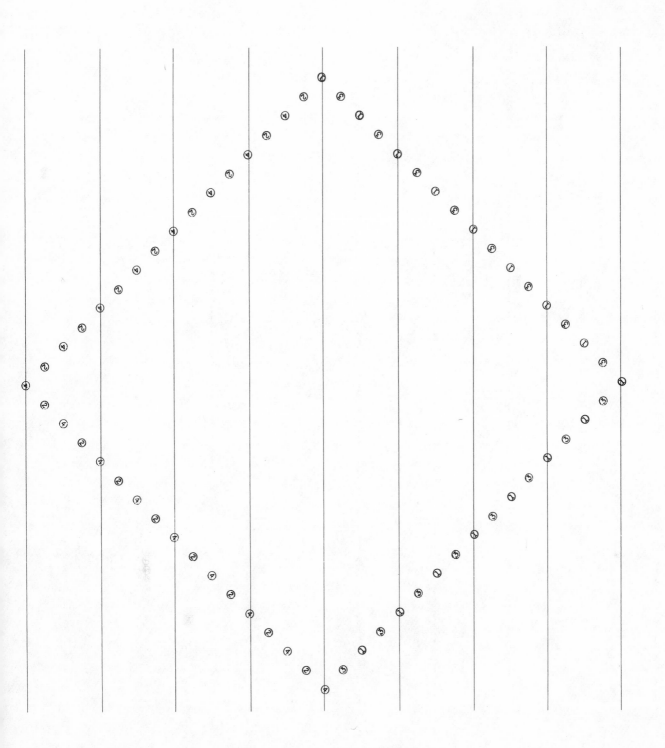

FIGURE 485—The movement is complete.

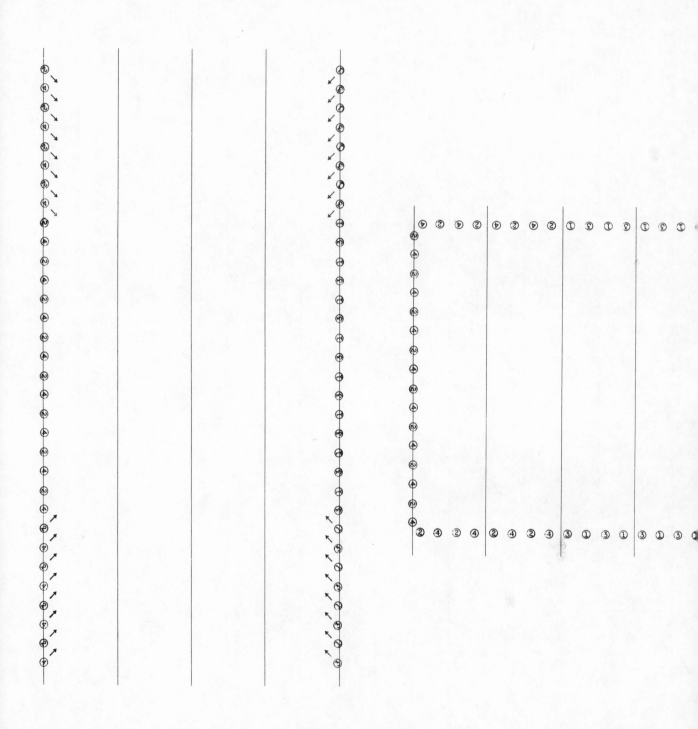

FIGURE 486—Each row is divided into three sections. The outside sections oblique on to a new line.

FIGURE 487—The movement is complete.

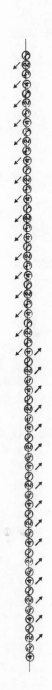

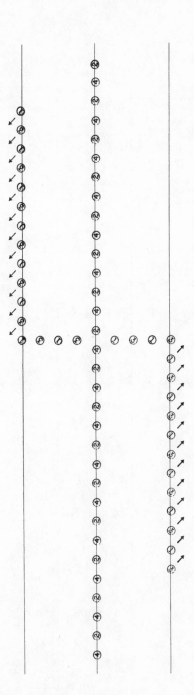

FIGURE 488—The ones and threes oblique on to a new line.

FIGURE 489—The movement continues.

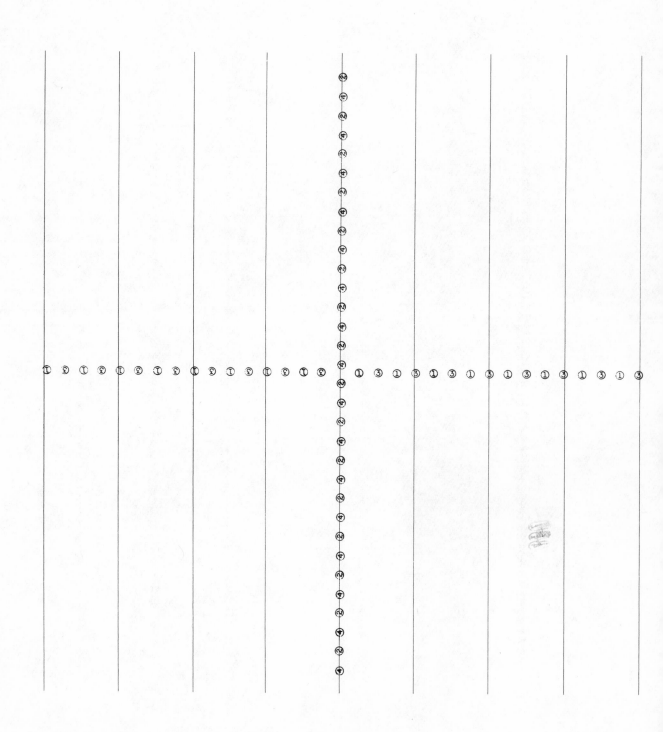

FIGURE 490—The movement is complete.

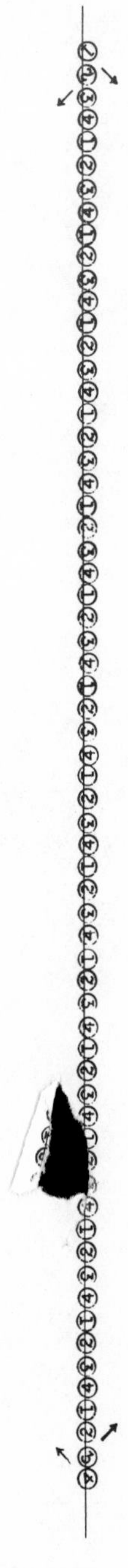

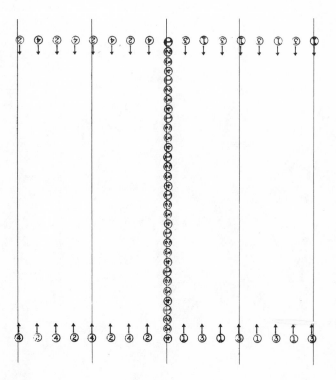

FIGURE 491—The meshed line is divided into three sections. The outside sections oblique to line.

FIGURE 492—The obliquing lines turn and move toward each other and mesh.

Sub-Formations

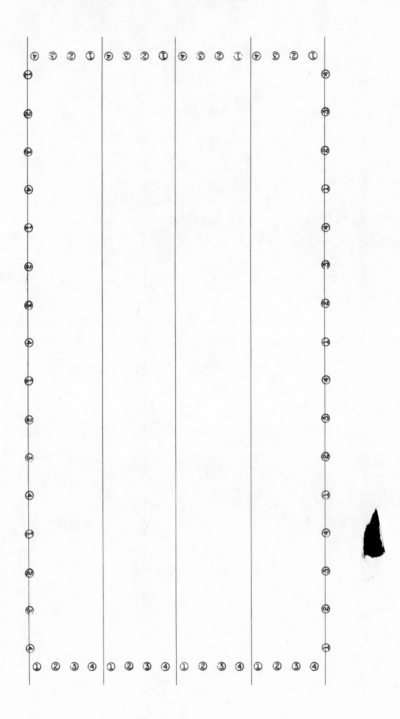

FIGURE 493—The rectangle is a good sub-formation for the letters—B, C, D, E, F, G, H, K, O, P,
Q, R, S, U, and Z.

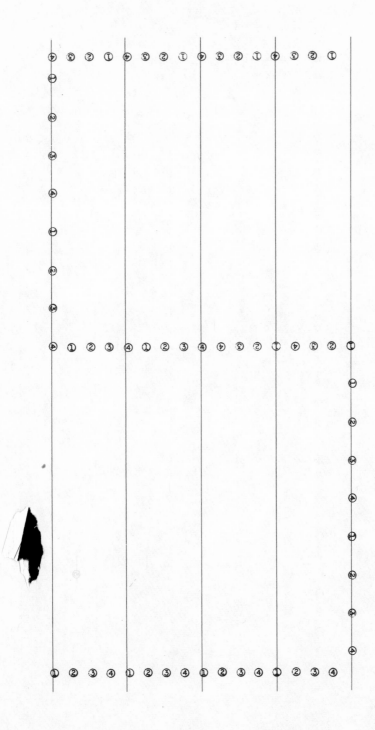

FIGURE 494—The letter "S" is executed from the rectangle by obliquing half of each side to form center bar.

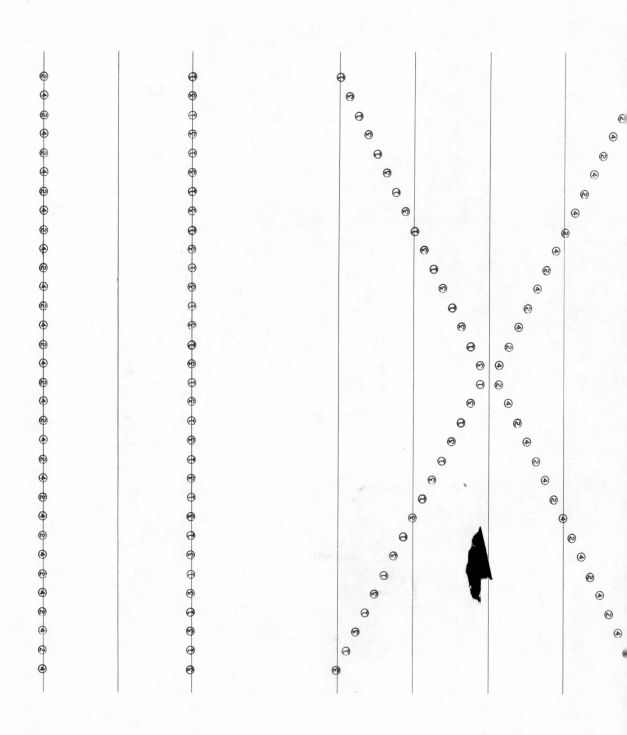

FIGURE 495—The double line is a good sub-formation for symmetrical letters.

FIGURE 496—The letter "X" is executed from the double line by a step 2, moving through the other line adjusting and moving into position.